GET THE JOB
Done ✔

118 Career Tips, Tools, and Internet Resources

Beverly A. Williams

Foreword by Ronald M. Green

Illustrations by Aaron Wms
Cartoon Artwork by Lyman Dally

Your Employment Matters

© 2013 by Parthenon Enterprises, Inc. (Your Employment Matters)

Library of Congress Control Number: 2013941756

ISBN: 978-0-9889837-1-7

"GPS to Employment Success" is the registered trademark of Parthenon Enterprises, Inc.

Proofreading and interior design by Joanne Shwed, Backspace Ink (www.backspaceink.com)

*This book is dedicated to my mother Rosa Lee,
and the memories of my father Clifford
and my godmother Vera:*

For all the lessons you taught me.

Contents

General Information

This book is provided as a practical guide and resource for general information on employment-related issues. While the author, editor, and publisher have made efforts to assure the accuracy of the material in this book as of February 1, 2013,[1] it should not be treated as a basis for formulating business and legal decisions without individualized legal advice. In legal matters, no publication can take the place of professional advice given with full knowledge of the specific circumstances of each matter and the actual practices of the employer.

This book contains links to third-party websites ("External Sites"). These links are provided solely as a convenience to you and not as an endorsement by us of the content on such External Sites. The content of such External Sites is developed and provided by others. You should contact the site administrator or webmaster for those External Sites if you have any concerns regarding such links or any content located on such External Sites.

We are not responsible for the content of any linked External Sites and do not make any representations regarding the content or accuracy of materials on such External Sites. You should take precautions when downloading files from all websites to protect your computer from viruses and other destructive programs. If you decide to access linked External Sites, you do so at your own risk.

The author, editor, and publisher make no representation or warranty, express or implied, as to the completeness, correctness, or utility of the information contained in this book and assume no liability of any kind whatsoever resulting from the use or reliance upon its contents. The references and advice are provided based on professional experiences and observations, and should be considered along with the reader's individual circumstances.

Foreword

At last, a sensible, practical, and instructive work on how to survive and succeed in corporate America—a must-read for those new to the game or simply stuck on the treadmill of corporate life.

Not surprisingly, this manual for success comes from the pen of a multifaceted attorney and human resource professional who has seen it all. She leads the reader through the fog of life as a job seeker and employee trying to make the most of opportunities available (if not always simply given), and it remains so apparent in the modern corporate world of work.

Beverly Williams clearly knows of what she speaks as she also brings her considerable skills and experience to bear, reminding the reader that taking charge of one's own life, riding out self-doubt, and believing in yourself make up the fuel that will propel the reader to new and unanticipated heights of achievement.

Armed with the best education you can get, the unique life experiences you have had, and aware of the extraordinary opportunities that lie ahead, let Beverly Williams teach you how to put it all together—as she has so ably done here.

—Ronald M. Green
Senior Partner
Epstein Becker & Green, P.C.
New York, New York

Preface

How would your life be different if ... you stopped
worrying about things you can't control and
started focusing on the things you can?

—Steve Maraboli, speaker, author, personal
coach, and national radio show host

In the New Employment Reality, a successful career is the individual's responsibility rather than the responsibility of employers, educational institutions, parents, or friends. There was a time when people used to go to school, get a job, and keep that job for life or get another one without a problem, but no longer. Now that it isn't as easy as it once was to get hired, it's up to job seekers to train themselves to land a job by distinguishing themselves from the competition.

Keeping the job or getting promoted is another matter, because employers can, among other things, decide to eliminate positions, thereby limiting the jobs and promotional opportunities available.

Whether you are looking for a new job or are just getting back into the workforce, you're bound to run into some surprises. My goal is to close the information gap by identifying common errors and offering the advice that I wish I'd had when I first began (and later changed) my career.

Get the Job • Done ✓ is designed to empower you to become the most successful job candidate or employee you can be. The first and second sections, "Getting Ready" and "Logistics & Self-Awareness," will be useful particularly for those of you who are just beginning your job searches because you are either unemployed or employed but looking for another opportunity. The objective is to prepare you for your employment journey and put you in a state of mind that allows you to consider, if not accept, the information and advice offered.

Section III, "Job Search 101," describes the work involved in looking for a job, and Section IV, "Career Planning & Advice," shows you how to move up with your current employer—or move on and up with a new employer. The last section, "More to Consider," addresses legal topics—your rights as well as your employer's rights—along with some personal issues.

Of course, the definition of a successful career varies from person to person, but it's something for which most of us strive. My hope is that *Get the Job • Done* ✓ will give you the necessary tools to achieve the level of success you choose—and beyond.

Sincere regards,

Acknowledgements

To my childhood friend Diane Williams Harris, who suggested that I write this book, thank you.

To the following people for their contributions and support, and whose encouraging words gave me the confidence to move forward:
"Ladies Who Lunch": Elena Rosellen, Debbie Morris, and particularly Nancy Poignant for her editorial support
Illene Ocampo, Barbara Miller, and Maria Tabone
Adrienne Colotti and Carolyn Powell
Raymond L. Colotti , Mary Guess Flamer, Kelly Makins Baugh, and Shelby Venson
John P. Barry, Patrick C. Daniel, and Justin Powell
Iris Carter Ford, Marsha Henderson, and Anaia Henderson
"The Style and Profile Quartet": Barbara Ealim, Julie Lane-Hailey, and Elaine Nelson
Gloria Bryant, Cayce Cummins, Valerie Boseman, and Michelle Ramirez Lopez
David L. Harris, Karim G. Kaspar, and Matt Savare
Brad Roth and Dansby White
Clifford A. Williams, Jr., Cynthia T. Williams, and Alexis M. Jones

Special thanks to Dieter Rosellen, Commander at VFW, Morris County, New Jersey; David R. Sperry, Staff Sergeant, United States Army; and John A. Bohichik, Transition Services Manager, Army Career & Alumni Program (NE Regional Office).

Introduction

You deserve to know why you should consider following my advice, so let me introduce myself.

My background: I grew up in a pro-union household because my father was a union official and my mother a union member. My respect for the efforts of organized labor is hard-wired and part of my DNA, but to my father's chagrin, as a labor-relations executive before I went to law school and after I became an attorney, I represented the management side of labor negotiations. As a legal consultant now, I also advise attorneys who represent labor unions.

I've worked in management and nonmanagement positions, and in union and nonunion environments. I've been employed in a direct-mail factory to run a paper-sorting machine; as a college-student counselor; as a human resources specialist in a large urban municipality, a large East Coast university, and a quasi-private, bistate agency; as a human resources and labor-relations executive in a large urban school district; as an attorney at a national labor and employment law firm; and as a lecturer and an author. My career goal was to become a vice president in a Fortune 500 company, and I achieved my goal.

My diverse employment history has given me the opportunity to work with a wide variety of people of different ages, races, genders, sexual orientations, and ethnicities. I'm not a parent but, on occasion, I'm called upon by my friends, their children, and sometimes their older friends and relatives to coach and mediate career matters. I know what they're going through, and I want to share what I've learned.

Why this book, and why now? Right now, many people are angry, frustrated, and frightened because they know that the employment situation has changed, but they may not fully grasp how extensive or permanent the change is and what they should do to make sure they can provide for themselves and their loved ones.

People who have always worked are unemployed or underemployed and struggling or unable to make ends meet. Those who have jobs may suffer from survivor's guilt because they weren't discharged or laid off. They may also be anxious about whether their employment will continue and what the future holds for them. Their concern is justified.

We've all seen and heard news reports about people adversely affected by the economy and the changes in the employment landscape. Their faces and stories touched me, like the tragic stories associated with Hurricane Katrina in 2005 and Super Storm Sandy in 2012.

I could do precious little to help those victims, but I can help empower people who have employment issues. This book and my website, www.youremploymentmatters.com, are tools you can use to successfully navigate what I call the "New Employment Reality," whether you have little or no work experience or have so much experience in one area that it's difficult to transition into another.

There is a wealth of information out there about how to find a job and how to manage your career, but this wealth of information can be overwhelming. How do you determine which blogger, author, or other employment expert has advice you should consider? Apart from guidance, suggestions, or recommendations, neither your technological proficiency nor your wisdom will be enough to evaluate the huge amount of free employment-related material available on the Internet. How do you know where to start?

My objective was to write a book that would provide much-needed information to a variety of people at different levels of their careers, and I wasn't afraid to ask for help. I elicited feedback from adults of all ages, ethnicities, and backgrounds at various stages of their careers. Not only did I receive relevant feedback, I also expanded my network and established what I hope will become enduring relationships.

I recognize that improving the economic picture and creating jobs are beyond the control of most people, but there are aspects of your employment situation over which you do have control. Most individuals at some time in their lives will have an interest in employment advice.

Why? Quite simply, at some point, almost all of us have to work, regardless of where we're from, what religion we follow, or whether we have a disability that may be debilitating but doesn't prevent us from earning a living.

You'll notice that I occasionally refer to sports teams and media programming. It doesn't matter what teams you follow or which way you lean on current issues. It also doesn't matter if you want to be a plumber, a doctor, a manager, a lab technician, a lawyer, or an executive. We all have the same goals. We want to impress decision makers enough to be hired. We hope that our supervisors will be impressed enough to promote us and increase our compensation.

Of course, there is always workplace etiquette to learn regardless of whether you think your position is permanent or temporary, and whether you work in an office or a factory. There is also etiquette to follow to receive the job offer in the first place. Although in some fields technology drives the recruiting process, other aspects of achieving employment success either haven't changed or have changed only slightly; old-fashioned manners are still key.

A few more considerations: You'll notice that tips and references may appear more than once, sometimes for emphasis and sometimes because they deserve mention under more than one topic. The tips may seem simple and more like common sense than professional advice, but something one person takes for granted might never occur to another person. Although the references and advice provided are based on professional experiences and observations, they should be considered along with the reader's individual circumstances.

Full disclosure: I admit that for more than one reason I haven't always followed the advice I now give. The primary reason is simple: ignorance. I wasn't aware of the rules that applied in the workplace. I didn't realize, as I do now, that there are universal rules as well as specific rules that evolve over time from different business cultures and different ways of doing things. I wasn't always aware of the employment "do's and don'ts," which shows you that education isn't enough, skills aren't enough, networks alone aren't enough, and intelligence isn't enough.

All these things help, but I learned from trial and error, and from people who mentored me later in my career, that in this job market, you need more.

SECTION I

Getting Ready

CHAPTER ONE

Don't Get Shot by a Bullet Labeled "To Whom It May Concern"

The true secret of giving advice is, after you have honestly given it, to be perfectly indifferent whether it is taken or not and never persist in trying to set people right.

—Hannah Whitall Smith, American evangelist[2]

[1] **Get advice from people you respect and who are knowledgeable.**

☑ Robert is a brilliant financier who is highly regarded in the business community. He makes time to mentor executives, those who aspire to be executives, and those in between.

A company that Robert knew intimately was undergoing a turbulent reorganization and cultural change. Several of the company's employees were Robert's friends, and they asked him to have lunch with them to discuss business developments and their thoughts on what some of the changes would be.

During lunch, Robert very smoothly leaned across the table, ran his gaze across each person's face, and told them to "do your job, mind your business, and keep your head down. It would be a shame for any of you to stick up your head and get shot by a bullet labeled 'to whom it may concern.'"

At first, Robert's friends didn't understand. They all were solid performers with (they thought) reasonably secure jobs. Then it dawned on one of them what Robert was telling them: While they might not be on a layoff list, that could change at any time, for any reason. That's why he was telling them not to draw attention to themselves and to stay under the radar. When they finally "got it," they realized that their jobs could be at risk.

While they stayed under the radar, they considered their options. Some of them chose to stay with the company while one chose to accept another employment opportunity. Of those who chose to remain with the company, only one person regretted his decision.

Robert's friends learned invaluable lessons. First, no matter how well you perform or think you perform, job security is an oxymoron—a contradiction in terms. Most jobs are not secure. Second, don't take anything for granted. For reasons unknown to you, and over which you have no control, your employment situation can change in the blink of an eye. You can change from hero to zero or, as one supervisor put it, from sugar to sh*t, in a New York minute. This is another reason to save money when you're employed.

2   Follow sound advice unless you have a good reason not to do so.

You'll probably receive advice from many different people—some who know what they're talking about and others not so much. Don't forget to exercise due diligence to determine whether the advice given by others and in this book works for you and your situation. That is, before you make a decision, check the reliability of your source and be objective.

Questions you might ask yourself include the following: What do you know about the person? Is he successful by your standards? Does she have the background—i.e., education and work experience—that makes her knowledgeable?

If you don't know the person offering advice, check out his or her bona fides or credentials to confirm that the advice offered at least has some credible basis to justify your consideration. Beware of those who claim to have all the answers. If possible, look for breadth and depth of experience and increasing levels of responsibilities.

I don't have all the answers, but as someone with work experience in nearly every sector of employment, who has held jobs with various and increasing levels of responsibility, and who has hired, supervised, evaluated, and discharged individuals, I do have a unique background. I have had the good fortune to work with people employed in white-collar, blue-collar, pink-collar, creative, building trades, service, manufacturing, and healthcare roles and industries. They have taught me well, and I have listened and learned.

You've probably already gone online for advice. The wealth of free information and free or inexpensive self-analytic tools on the Internet can help you identify your career path or occupation, and provide guidance about other employment matters.

At the end of this book, in the Resources section of the Career Toolkit, and at the end of some of the chapters, there are links to third-party websites that you might find useful. Keep in mind that access to free material often requires you to view numerous ads along the way. In addition, some websites offer only enough free information to convince you to purchase their product.

3   Manage your expectations.

4   Make sure your expectations are realistic.

As you begin to look for work, take a deep breath and prepare yourself for the task ahead. You should set reasonable expectations so you don't become discouraged if you don't find a job immediately.

If your job search is directed toward a job for which you are qualified, and you are able to persuasively articulate the value you bring and why you should be hired, your hard work should pay off. If you do your homework (which includes researching the employer), dress appropriately for the interview, and do not commit any faux pas (like making seemingly innocent but inappropriate remarks about how much alcohol you consume on the weekend), and there are no background-check issues, you should achieve a favorable result.

If, however, you are applying for jobs for which you are not qualified and you handle your job search in a cavalier fashion, save your time. No one will hire you in this job market unless they have to because you are related to someone to whom they owe a huge favor. In a recession, returning a favor may not be adequate incentive to hire an unqualified candidate.

You will likely get from your employment search what you put into it in terms of, among other things, time, effort, follow-up, networking, job-board searches, and résumés. Persistence and tenacity are essential to achieving positive results; without them, you will not likely be successful.

If you are employed, it's important that what you expect as an employee and what your supervisor expects from you are in sync. Your expectations and those of your supervisor also should be reasonable, realistic, and attainable given internal and external circumstances and factors.

Make no mistake: It's your responsibility to make sure that you clearly understand what is expected of you, and when and where you must deliver what is requested. Your supervisor isn't obligated to take responsibility or back you up if you don't meet his or her expectations. If you are fairly compensated for work performed, there is a fair exchange. You should not expect more unless you contribute more and deserve it. In time, you'll recognize opportunities and learn to seize them when they are presented.

INCONVENIENT TRUTHS

Some of your habits, behaviors, opinions, and social mores might be endearing to your friends and family but not to your employer. You may have to set them aside in order to find a job and be successful on the job once you're hired. The people you'll need to impress to get a job or promotion may have an "old-school" mindset.

Can you live with a more conservative you, at least during working hours and for work-related events? Only you have the answer.

5 You don't know what you don't know and why you don't know it.

This tip sounds like double talk, but it isn't. Often in a work environment, information is disseminated in measured doses on a need-to-know basis. No matter how talented you are, how gifted you may be, or how brilliant you've been told you are, you won't be privy to information that, for example, is above your position or pay grade.

6 Seek information, not affirmation.

Unbiased information is powerful; if nothing else, it enables you to make informed decisions. Regardless of what kind of job you're seeking, you'll need objective feedback about who you are and what value you can bring to an employer. By definition, family and friends are not objective about you and your talents. Input from an eclectic group of people you can rely on to give you constructive feedback is not only important, it's essential.

If you can, find men and women of various ages, ethnicities, religions, and sexual orientations, along with professionals employed in a multitude of functions, who know you well enough to be helpful as you plan your career. If you can't amass such a group, do the best you can with the people you know. Going forward, your efforts to expand your network base and make it as varied as possible will only help.

7 To your loved ones, you may be all that and a bag of chips but, in the workplace, you're an employee and a coworker.

Depending on how involved your loved ones are in the different aspects of your life, you may have to have a polite but firm conversation with them. As much as they want to help, they are looking at you through rose-colored glasses. They also might not know where to interfere and when to step aside. If you decide to have a talk with them, you should:

- Acknowledge their love and good intentions.

- Assure them that you need their help to make networking contacts, practice your marketing pitch to prospective employers, and prepare for interviews.

- Tell them that, if you don't follow their advice, this doesn't mean that you don't appreciate or respect it.

8 Your family members aren't always right, but they're not always wrong.

☑ Carolyn, who has a Master of Business Administration (MBA) from a prestigious business school, didn't give her son the appropriate advice. Carolyn's son Jason is a junior in college who wants to pursue a career as a sports writer. Through his networking contacts, Jason was given a courtesy interview with Jonah, a sports writer with an online column and blog. Jason appropriately

planned to send Jonah an e-mail to thank him for his time and the information he provided. Carolyn was appalled. She directed Jason to purchase a card
so that he could send a handwritten thank-you via snail mail.

The type of thank-you depends on the person to whom you're
sending it. Online columnists and bloggers are digital people. An
e-mail thank-you is acceptable and may be preferred by people like
Jonah who work remotely and communicate electronically. Jason was
right. Although Carolyn's intentions were good, and a thank-you note
was appropriate, her advice was wrong.

☑ Rosa and her husband Javier planned to attend a social event hosted
by Javier's manager at a local restaurant, but Rosa had a job interview the
afternoon of the event. To save time, Javier said that he would drive her to
the job interview and wait for her in the reception area.

Javier was correct to want to save time, but Rosa knew that, if her well-
meaning husband accompanied her to the interview, it would appear unprofessional and inappropriate. Rosa gently yet firmly explained this to Javier
and suggested that he wait for her at a nearby coffee shop.

If you're looking for your first job, chances are that your parents,
aunts, uncles, and friends of the family know more people than you
do because they've lived and worked longer. If you're looking to get
back into the job market, your children, grandchildren, nieces, and
nephews might know people on their social networking sites who are
hiring and put you in touch with them; they can also help you with
technology if you're uncomfortable with it. Even if your network is
robust, it won't hurt to sit down with your family and come up with a
list of all the people in your combined networks.

9   Select and maintain relationships thoughtfully and wisely.

In Chapter Six, you're going to be asked to think about who will
accompany you on your employment journey. Go ahead and begin a

mental list of loved ones, friends, family members, coaches, instructors, and the other people you know whom you might include on your list, and why. Ideally, this list will be the start of a network that will grow and serve you well in the future.

| 10 | You can dress, talk, and conduct yourself as you choose, but be prepared to accept the consequences.

Fortunately, we live in a country of free speech and freedom of choice; however, as a job applicant or an employee, you might have to make decisions about whether to exercise your right to assert your individuality. Are you willing to wear less flamboyant clothing and not have unusual hair colors and hairstyles? Are you willing to keep your opinions about politics, religion, and other potentially controversial subjects to yourself?

Your personal appearance and behavior on and off the job can impact whether you get hired and whether your career has an upward trajectory after you're hired. The way you think things *should* be may not be the way things *are*; many times, the only reason for the difference is the idiosyncrasy of the business or supervisor.

For example, the company you work for allows facial hair on men and open-toe shoes for women, but your manager is an "old-school," forty-year-old who makes it clear that she thinks beards, moustaches, and peep-toe pumps are inconsistent with the conservative business image your employer wants to project.

Seriously, there are traditional companies that favor a more restrained style and share your manager's point of view. What do you do? Do you exercise your right, wear what you want, and possibly annoy your boss when you do, or do you conform? Fortunately, you have a choice, but you also have a decision to make.

11   Don't hate the player; hate the game.

Until you master how to play the employment game, you may envy or even resent people who play it well. Proficiency is achieved through experience and learning from personal mistakes and the mistakes of others, and not repeating them. Respect the results achieved by individuals who play the game well and with integrity, and master the game yourself.

Larry is a good example. He always volunteers for overtime and contributes to special projects regularly with a smile and a pleasant word to everyone. Everyone likes Larry, but some coworkers resent his recent promotion. My advice is to replace resentment with imitation. If you were Larry's coworker, I'd suggest that you spend more time with Larry to learn from him and to give him an opportunity to learn from you.

I'd also suggest that you find time to volunteer for projects. It's an opportunity to meet people and hopefully acquire information. If you take my advice, perhaps you'll be on your way to distinguishing yourself like Larry.

12   Consider all feedback a gift, and learn to accept negative feedback without becoming defensive.

Constructive feedback almost always includes both positive and negative information, some of which you may agree with and some you may not. If you don't receive negative feedback well, you'll need to practice accepting it as you would accept an ugly gift from a loved one. How well you handle feedback may be a factor when recruiters debrief you after an interview and when your supervisor gives you your annual performance review.

If you solicit feedback, be sure to accept it graciously, even if you don't agree with it. Consider it a gift, one that makes you smile, because it will help you improve. At the very least, feedback may give you information you may not have had about the person who gives it, especially if you had assumed that the person was your supporter.

People we thought were in our corner might not show it in their feedback, and others might be more generous with their feedback than we expected. Before you conclude that people who only give you negative feedback are not supportive, consider whether they have experience giving feedback. Do they know that constructive feedback is generally delivered by giving positive comments first followed by less favorable, temperate comments? You might want to confirm that they know this before judging them too harshly.

13   Don't shoot the messenger.

Like feedback, information you receive at work may be positive or negative, and conveyed by someone who may or who may not mean you well, such as a human resources (HR) manager or assistant. Regardless, don't react negatively toward the person who delivers the message or information. It's simply bad form. Furthermore, that person may be someone you'll meet again in the future, and he or she may recall—to your detriment—how you handled yourself.

14   Have a positive attitude.

Simply put, no one wants to help a person with a bad attitude.

☑   Nicole didn't graduate from college and didn't get good grades in high school, but she somehow always finds a job. She has changed jobs for personal reasons several times and, each time she needed to find another job, someone hired her.

Why? Nicole's references are effusive in their praise of her interpersonal relationship skills, work ethic, and reliability. People consistently describe her as having "a nice way about her." She always has a smile, never has a negative attitude, works hard, gets the job done, and is always on time for work.

Like Larry, Nicole is someone to emulate.

15 You're not better than anyone else, and no one is better than you are.

America is a democracy where all people are considered equal. Some employers seem to have an egalitarian work environment where executives are called by their first names and "business casual" is the policy-designated dress code. It may appear that everyone is equal in the workplace, but don't be fooled; they really aren't. Don't make the mistake of becoming too familiar and too comfortable with your supervisor and other employees in higher positions.

It's wise to maintain a level of professionalism and self-respect. Someone will notice. You never know when you'll have an opportunity to present yourself and your career goals to someone who can help you or knows someone who can. That said, you should always be "on" and bring your "A" game.

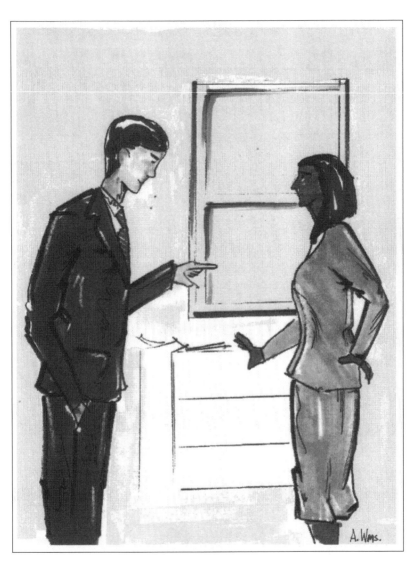

Consider all feedback a gift.

CHAPTER TWO

The New Employment Reality ... The Fairy Tale Is Over!

*One of the great liabilities of history is that all too many
people fail to remain awake through great periods of social
change. Every society has its protectors of status quo and
its fraternities of the indifferent who are notorious for
sleeping through revolutions. Today, our very survival
depends on our ability to stay awake, to adjust to new ideas,
to remain vigilant and to face the challenge of change.*

—Martin Luther King, Jr., minister, social
activist, and civil rights leader

Once upon a time ...

- Numerous employers considered their employees "family"
  and adopted a paternalistic approach to managing their
  workforces.

- Likewise, employees considered themselves members of
  the "family" and trusted their employers to act in their best
  interests.

- People who worked decades for the same company were
  respected and highly regarded, and enjoyed job security.

■ In many instances, it was considered disloyal to even think about looking for a job with another employer, especially a competitor.

■ In return for long years of service, satisfactory performance, and loyalty, employees were often promoted and received annual salary increases.

■ Employees recruited their family members and friends to work for the company, and they also became long-term employees.

■ Working for one company until retirement became a family tradition.

Whether you're employed or unemployed, you've felt the seismic shift in the employment landscape either directly or indirectly. You know that the fairy tale is over!

16 | Accept that there is a New Employment Reality, and embrace it.

The mutual loyalty and trust that employers and their employees shared are no longer commonplace. As far too many employees today have learned, loyalty and trust, while important, aren't always reciprocal. Their jobs have been eliminated or moved to another country or state because of business decisions that favored outsourcing, restructuring, and maximizing profitability.

Consequently, you're going to need to think differently about employment. Why? It's simple. There is a New Employment Reality, and it doesn't remotely resemble your parents' or grandparents' employment experiences.

Perhaps the one factor that has remained constant in the ever-changing employment arena is that success is driven first and foremost by the individual. As employees and prospective employees, you'll need to plan and manage your employment future with your eyes on global and industry developments.

Early in his first term, President Barack Obama delivered what should be a wake-up call for American workers, and warned that the world has changed. The president reminisced:

> Many people ... probably remember a time when finding a good job meant showing up at a nearby factory or a business downtown. You didn't always need a degree, and your competition was pretty much limited to your neighbors. If you worked hard, chances are you'd have a job for life, with a decent paycheck and good benefits and the occasional promotion. Maybe you'd even have the pride of seeing your kids work at the same company.[3]

President Obama's message doesn't appear to resonate with American workers as emphatically as it should in light of various factors that drive business decisions, including hiring needs. Some time ago, an item on the Internet ("Changes Are Coming" by Clark McClelland, http://rense.com/general92/goodbye.htm) detailed not only business changes brought about by technology, but it also forecast additional changes that will radically alter how business will be conducted in the future. The e-mail identified the U.S. Post Office, newspapers, land-line telephones, books, checks, music, and television as glaring examples of businesses and aspects of businesses that have been undeniably and permanently altered.

It's obvious how technology has changed businesses but, for some, it's difficult to accept that land lines and post offices may become a distant memory.

More change is coming because:

- E-mail usage has increased.

- The use of snail mail has declined.

- Cell phones and social media have increased as the preferred choice of communication for many.

- Purchasing e-books, banking online, and acquiring news and music online have increased.

- Multiple platforms are available for viewing and listening to media programming.

The technological changes that drove the business changes have also affected the types of jobs and number of workers needed to perform those jobs in related businesses, but there is no need to panic. The situation isn't as bad as it may sound. The United States has been through this before. Remember the Industrial Revolution? The country gradually but successfully transitioned from an agrarian to an industrial society.

As the need to transition arises again, people may need to reconsider how they handle their employment matters and the advice they give their children. Aggressively managing their careers, proactively creating multiple income streams, and keeping abreast of industry developments are just a few examples of what achieving employment success will require in the future.

Just as everyday people have had to adapt to changes in how they look for a job and accept the disappearance of job security, the owners of professional sports franchises, sports agents, and professional basketball coaches find themselves confronted by a change in who does business in their world and how. Thanks to LeBron James and

Jay-Z, the New Employment Reality has now arrived on the doorstep of professional sports.

LeBron's departure from the Cleveland Cavaliers for the Miami Heat in July 2010 is a template for how to manage a career:

■ Set goals.

■ Be an excellent performer.

■ Give yourself a reasonable amount of time within which to achieve your goals, and factor in your talent and marketability.

LeBron made a boatload of money in Cleveland, but he had reasonable, achievable career goals. He not only wanted to be on a championship team, he also wanted to win the National Basketball Association (NBA) championship for multiple years. Sure, LeBron left Cleveland (to play for Miami for less money) without bringing an NBA championship to that city, but he gave it seven seasons.

LeBron felt that moving to Miami would give him the best opportunity to achieve his career goals. He was right. With back-to-back successes, the Miami Heat is the NBA's 2013 and 2012 Championship Team. Career goals one and two ... Done ✓ and Done ✓!

Don't get it twisted: Don't delude yourself about your talents and marketability. Compare LeBron's approach to his career with how Eve—an experienced, mature HR professional—handled her job search.

☑ Several years ago, Eve resigned as Director of Human Resources of a prominent teaching hospital because she was tired of working. After two years, Eve decided that she missed the interaction with people, and wanted to return to work. It was no surprise that Eve was called in for interviews by most of the companies at which she applied because her résumé was impressive, and she had the desired pedigree. Her educational background included undergraduate and graduate degrees, and she had extensive industry work experience.

When Eve arrived for a series of interviews at a large healthcare organization, based on her polished appearance and professional demeanor, the staffing coordinator concluded that Eve could be the total package. The staffing coordinator was correct. Eve was intelligent, articulate, and knowledgeable about the HR profession.

Before Eve left for the day, the hiring manager told her they were close to making a decision among the top three applicants, one of whom was Eve. Inexplicably, Eve felt compelled to inform him quite candidly and unequivocally that she only wanted to work four days a week, and that she wanted Fridays off. In her opinion, any job could be performed in four days.

The hiring manager told Eve that she would hear from the staffing coordinator.

Guess what? She is still waiting for the call that will never come.

Unlike LeBron, Eve overestimated her value on the open market. Another difference between them is that LeBron was in the position to create a New Employment Reality for himself while Eve could only react to the New Employment Reality that had already been created.

You would think that, given her profession and experience, Eve would have known that there are many talented, unemployed HR professionals looking for jobs, and that no one (*especially* an HR professional) is irreplaceable. The moral of the story is that people of all ages overplay their hands. Please don't be one of them.

Nearly three years after LeBron left Cleveland, Jay-Z shook up things in the sports world of agents and agencies by extending his brand, business success, acumen, and passion to the representation of professional athletes. Roc Nation Sports, Jay-Z's new "full-service entertainment company," teamed with Creative Artists Association (CAA) to create what could become an eight-hundred-pound gorilla of negotiating prowess.

Notably, CAA already represents A-list musicians, actors, and athletes like Justin Timberlake, Meryl Streep, and LeBron James. Roc Nation Sports reportedly has begun its foray into Major League Baseball and the National Football League (NFL) by signing highly marketable talent like the New York Yankees' Robinson Cano and the New York Giants' Victor Cruz as clients. With news that Kevin Durant, NBA superstar of the Oklahoma City Thunder, has signed with Roc Nation Sports, expect to hear that more marquee NBA players are joining the Roc Nation Sports family.

There is also speculation about whether LeBron will leave CAA for Roc Nation Sports. Given the relationship between Jay-Z and CAA, don't be surprised if they work it out to all parties' mutual benefit. Of course, they may not, but you have to admit that Jay-Z's involvement makes things interesting.

The sports world should not be surprised to hear that other elite professional athletes have joined Roc Nation Sports, and not just athletes of color, as some sportscasters predict. At the very least, rookie and younger professional athletes are potential clients.

Ask anyone: Jay-Z transcends race. Trying to pigeonhole or otherwise limit him is fruitless. Jay-Z's superstardom and brand, along with his entrepreneurial savvy and influential contacts, translate into multidimensional, potentially lucrative business opportunities for his clients.

With Jay-Z at their side, the sky is the only ceiling on additional income streams that professional athletes can reasonably and realistically develop. The business opportunities beyond the sport in which they excel can be identified, explored, and nurtured under Jay-Z's expert watch.

Professional basketball coaches are also realizing that their employment future may now be driven by professional athletes who, because of their talent and star power, can influence hiring decisions.

Glenn "Doc" Rivers, former coach of the Boston Celtics, and Jason Kidd, former point guard for the New York Knicks, are now coaches for the Los Angeles Clippers and Brooklyn Nets, respectively, because marquee players have expressly or implicitly expressed their coaching preferences. If rumors are true, the Los Angeles Lakers lost Dwight Howard, their former star center, because he reportedly didn't like the Lakers coach's system and preferred to play a starring rather than a supporting role on the team.

Fans, owners, agents, and coaches may lament the changes, but some professional athletes evidently got the message that responsibility for planning a career, setting goals, and working toward achieving those goals must be shouldered by the individual, and they decided to take a more proactive role in managing their careers. Conventional wisdom suggests that professional sports-franchise owners, agents, and coaches should fasten their seatbelts because they could be in for an unsettling ride.

Admittedly, the average person doesn't have LeBron's or Jay-Z's talents, isn't as marketable, and is probably employed or looking for employment in a workplace more mundane than the NBA or Jay-Z's Roc Nation Sports. Jay-Z and LeBron nonetheless can be used to illustrate what it means to set career goals, manage a career, and create multiple income streams.

In the New Employment Reality, individuals can't rely on anyone else to chart the courses of their careers. Everyday people, who don't have the leverage that professional athletes have, still have options. Once they determine the career path that fits them best, they should set a course for success as they define it and work toward that goal.

There may be periods of unemployment but, by turning a passion, hobby, or interest into an income stream, people can earn money.

A temporary or part-time job is another way to make money while searching for full-time employment. Depending on the needs of the business and the person's performance, this option has the additional potential benefit of evolving into a full-time position.

Each day, a tremendous number of people vie for a limited number of jobs that didn't exist fifteen to twenty years ago. Consequently, be loyal to and trust yourself. Today, anyone looking for work or aspiring toward promotion should:

- Use all available resources aggressively and exhaustively;

- Take nothing for granted;

- Keep up their spirits; and

- Keep a sense of humor.

17 "Job security" is a contradiction in terms.

Economic downturns have caused us to focus on the high rate of unemployment and the substantial loss of jobs through attrition, restructuring, right-sizing, mergers and acquisitions, outsourcing, off-shoring, and right-shoring. In many instances, work performed by permanent, full-time employees is now performed by a cadre of temporary workers. Businesses that formerly operated in the United States have moved to foreign locations.

Consequently, long years of service aren't easy to achieve today and provide little if any job security. When you ask long-term employees who have been laid off and are unable to find comparable work, they are acutely aware that the employment landscape has changed.

By comparison, people who are employed and haven't otherwise been adversely impacted by the shift in the employment picture breathe a sigh of relief because they dodged a bullet—at least for the time being. Individuals, whether employed or unemployed, who are still in a work-for-the-same-employer-until-retirement state of mind, are likely in for a rude awakening.

☑ Twice each year, my friend Gloria invites me to be a guest lecturer for her business-law course, which is offered as part of a company's on-site training and development program. It's a somewhat informal group of approximately ten to fifteen private-sector, salaried, and hourly employees.

I always stick to the agenda because I want to make sure that students get what they signed up for, but I leave time to discuss employment generally. After I talk about the employee-employer relationship and the rights and obligations of each party, I engage the class in a discussion about how employment and businesses have changed and the New Employment Reality.

I then ask students, "Where do you see yourself in five and ten years?" Most students say they don't know; some say they haven't given it any thought.

A woman in her late thirties named Farha was memorable because she presented a clear description of her five-year plan for the future. Her plan included obtaining another degree and additional training to expand her skillset and make her more marketable.

She emphatically said, "If I have to take more time, I will, but I know what I want out of life." It was as if Farha used the LeBron James career template. She had a plan that contains realistic goals and a flexible timetable for achieving those goals, and she is executing her plan.

Barry, another person who stood out in my mind, was a pleasant young man who appeared to be in his late twenties or early thirties. He seemed excited about his career plans and eager to share them with the class.

Barry said, "I see myself working for my company until retirement because it's a great place to work, and there are numerous promotional opportunities." Barry worked for a large insurance company, which, like any other company, could become a merger or acquisition target.

Another young man named Clifford said roughly the same thing about his future plans. He was employed by an automobile manufacturer that is growing its market share but is not in the top ten of the industry's manufacturers.

Hopefully, the people who haven't even considered planning their futures will at least think about it. In my opinion, the young men who see themselves working for the same companies until retirement simply don't get it.

The American automobile industry has gone through a rough transition. The insurance industry may expand or contract because of healthcare issues and legislation. It's quite possible that, given the restructuring, mergers, and acquisitions that have become the new normal, the companies Barry and Clifford work for today may not even exist ten to twenty years from now.

18 Your employment matters are solely your responsibility.

Many employees realize they will need to switch careers at some stage in their life. Not only has the job-for-life disappeared, but the career-for-life is going the same way.
—Mike Webster, Kelly Services Executive
Vice President and General Manager

My point of view: It's time for individuals to be more proactive about employment. It was (and still is) common for employees to rely on employers' career-development initiatives, and to wait, sometimes for years, to be anointed by management and moved up through the company's hierarchy. Promotions and length of service were (and still are, in some companies) inextricably linked, and the resulting sense of entitlement became pervasive in the workplace.

It's not unusual for:

■ Workers to be promoted within their job classifications several years after they're hired, if they have performed just satisfactorily; and

■ Employees to wait years for another promotion, especially if they were promoted at least once since the day they were hired.

In a large company, a person could be promoted from analyst to senior analyst two, three, or four years after joining and not receive another promotion until five or six years later, if ever.

☑ David worked for a company for fifteen years without a promotion. He had been passed over for promotion several times and finally decided to file a complaint through his employer's complaint procedure.

When asked why he thought he should be promoted, David replied, "I've been employed for seventeen years. I was promoted two years after I was hired, and I always received satisfactory performance reviews."

He acknowledged that he didn't think there was a legal basis for his claim. David simply felt that he deserved a promotion, and he needed to make more money.

Notably, he wasn't the only long-term employee in his department who had been promoted only once. When asked why he hadn't looked for other opportunities within the company or at another company after fifteen years without a promotion, he didn't have an answer. Apparently, he not only felt entitled to be promoted, but it never occurred to him that he had other options.

David lost money by remaining in a position and waiting in vain to be promoted; he also felt undervalued and unappreciated. David may have done himself and his employer a favor by looking elsewhere, either internally or externally, for a position that he felt he deserved.

What David didn't know was that his company had decided years ago to sell his division. The only reason David's division remained part of the company was because a buyer had not been found.

Here are two "take aways" from David's scenario:

1. Absent some legal grounds like breach of contract, employees can't force employers to promote them. The power to promote rests with employers.

2. While David believed he deserved a promotion, whatever he was doing wasn't enough to make his employer reach for his or her wallet to promote him. Make sure you are as deserving as you think you are.

If you're employed: Employees should question whether they can afford to remain on the same job and be a loyal employee if they feel unappreciated and undervalued, especially when there is no indication that they will be promoted again.

Given the impact of technological advances, and the power that employers have to send jobs elsewhere and to reorganize their businesses, there is no guarantee as to how long positions will exist or remain where they are currently located. Thus, employees don't know whether they'll be retained in their present positions. Their wishing and hoping won't change that reality.

If you're unemployed: The truth is that, during a recession, high unemployment and underemployment put employers in the driver's seat. They have a wealth of candidates from which to select to fill vacancies. Their employees may not be thrilled with their current positions, but they are grateful to have jobs.

According to a *Business Week* article:

> Employers are trying to get rid of all fixed costs. First they did it with employment benefits. Now they're doing it with the jobs themselves. Everything is variable. That means companies hold all the power, and all the risks are pushed on to employees.[4]

Given the severity of the recession, the conventional wisdom is that a shift in the bargaining power in favor of employees is a long way off. To add insult to injury, at least from the job seeker's perceptive:

- There are many competent, well-educated, highly skilled, experienced people who are looking for employment opportunities.

- Compensation levels can be suppressed because there are so many people looking for work.

- Some employers may offer to pay less because someone will accept the lower salary.

Don't believe for one minute that every employer will pay top dollar to attract and hire talent when a competent person is available to do the job and will do it for less money. It's business, and it's a buyer's market.

Now more than ever, individuals have to:

- Become better informed about their employer's and prospective employer's industry;

- Become tactfully aggressive and persistent with their job searches;

- Be nimble and flexible about pursuing other employment options, such as relocating to another state or country; and

- Create additional revenue streams by following their passions or interests early in their career.

☑ Michael was a high school senior who loved to play video games and was quite good at it. He started to play in junior high school, when he created his own online channel. Michael created videos of his game-playing and began uploading them to YouTube.

After about two years, Michael's channel had attracted a robust following, as evidenced by the impressive number of hits he received. As a result of his gaming proficiency and considerable following of like-minded gamers, Michael attracted the attention of a team that uploaded videos on YouTube under the team's name.

Advertisers pay Google to advertise on its sites, so the more traffic Google can generate, the better for both the advertiser and Google. For three years while Michael was in high school, Google paid the team that Michael was on, and the team paid Michael based on the number of hits his videos got.

If he chooses, Michael can continue to generate income while he attends college. Now *that* is the kind of revenue stream to create! You get paid to do something you love and are good at, and that is fun. What could be better?

Don't get it twisted: Don't quit your job unless and until you have a written offer for another position. Quitting your job during a recession because the promotion or recognition you think you deserve hasn't materialized isn't the move to make.

INCONVENIENT TRUTHS

When the rate of unemployment is high and the economic forecast is promising—but uncertain—individuals looking for employment should prepare themselves for the work involved and evaluate their situations to determine whether a permanent lifestyle change is necessary.

Creating multiple revenue streams, turning a passion into a revenue-generating venture, and reinventing, rebranding, or redirecting themselves are examples of how creative people can be in trying times.

19 Acquiring a job is a competition.

Gainful employment is a state of being that many of us took for granted until recently. Few people probably ever asked the questions, "Is employment a right, a privilege, or something else completely? If I want to work, am I entitled to a job or position?"

Current circumstances drive home the fact that employment is neither a right nor a privilege. It is a competition. In fact, it has always been a competition, and fewer jobs mean more intense competition.

> The burden of proof has shifted to the job seeker to demonstrate value and fit ... Job seekers need to be bolder and more energetic in this very challenging market. They need to show that they're willing to go above and beyond and that they'll work hard, tirelessly and take initiative to get the job done ... It's not enough to say, "Here I am." The emphasis is now on, "Here's what I can do for you."[5]

20 Finding a job in the New Employment Reality requires work.

Wanting and needing a job won't get you hired. You'll need to research the industry in which you're interested in working because the materials you submit and your clothing will be different for corporate, creative, building trades, or nonprofit employment opportunities. Identify the geographical locations where there are available jobs and where there are the most jobs in the largest area within commuting distance. There is more to be done, such as initiating and participating in networking activities; drafting résumés, marketing pitches, and cover and thank-you letters; and practicing interviewing skills.

21 Consider relocating to other states and countries to find employment.

If your research indicates that there are no jobs where you live or in nearby locations within commuting distance, and that isn't likely to change in the near future, relocation is an option. To make this option more reasonable to you and your loved ones, focus on communities where family members or friends live.

22 Be flexible about changing jobs and employers.

Employees should exercise their option to seek employment elsewhere within the company they work for, or externally if they don't receive promotions they think they legitimately deserve.

You may be doing such a good job in your current role that, for selfish reasons, your supervisor wants you to remain there. Unfortunately, not all supervisors are good leaders. Just remember: It's unwise to leave a job if you don't have another job.

It's not reasonable to expect a promotion if:

- You don't complete assignments satisfactorily and on schedule;

- Your attendance, including punctuality, is unsatisfactory;

- Your personal appearance, including personal hygiene, clothing, hairstyle, hair color, and fingernails, is inconsistent with your employer's business culture and image;

- You're constantly involved in workplace drama; and/or

- You have a "reason" for your shortcomings on the job. ("Reason" is code for "excuse.")

23 Keep your career goals and objectives fluid.

Absolutely follow your passion! Don't accept what people say you can't do, as long as you're willing to work hard to achieve your desired goal and have the requisite talent to do so.

Simultaneously, however, keep your eye on whether external forces, such as industry changes, make your desired goal unattainable or otherwise affect your plans. For example, if your dream job is in the automobile, entertainment, or media industries, which have undergone considerable changes, you may need to rethink your vision. You may still get your dream job, but you might have to wait, work longer, and take more risks to achieve it.

Rather than give up on your dream, move forward with determination. *You can do it!*

24 **Acquire more training, including a bachelor's degree (if you don't have one) or a graduate degree (if you have an undergraduate one) to expand your skillset.**

Regardless of your educational level, your research may disclose that you lack essential skills for available employment opportunities. In-person and online degrees and career-development certificate programs offered by local colleges and universities are options. Select training programs that will supplement and enhance your skillset. If you're unemployed, focus on employers that offer tuition assistance benefits; if you're employed, take advantage of this benefit if your employer offers it.

25 **Identify ways to create additional income streams.**

Some celebrities, who once upon a time were ordinary people, are particularly adept at creating multiple income streams.

Channel the following celebrities as you consider how to generate additional income:

- Anderson Cooper—journalist, television talk-show host, producer, and author

- Ellen DeGeneres—comedienne, television talk-show host, reality-show judge, cosmetics spokesperson, and actress

- Chelsea Handler—comedienne, television talk-show host, author, producer, and actress

- Heidi Klum—supermodel, television show host, entrepreneur, fashion designer, reality-show judge, producer, and actress

- Justin Timberlake—singer, actor, fashion designer, producer, and entrepreneur

- Wendy Williams—television talk-show host, actress, author, producer, and entrepreneur

- Jay-Z—rapper, record producer, film producer, actor, and entrepreneur

Anderson Cooper's multiple income streams appear to remain within his primary career of journalism, which makes him an interesting study. It's unusual for a journalist to be seen on different networks, but Cooper has successfully negotiated the freedom to appear prominently and regularly on CNN, on CBS's *60 Minutes*, and on ABC in 2007 as the substitute cohost of *Live with Regis and Kelly*. His talent, experience, and personal brand enable him to request the freedom he wants and receive it.

The celebrities listed above have positioned themselves by their hard work to have choices. Some of them have had career hiccups or setbacks, but the common themes are hard work and learning from experience.

You don't have to be a celebrity to create income streams. By turning a passion, hobby, or interest into a service or product that people need, you can generate extra money, if only a small amount at first.

Perhaps it's time to start your own business. If you haven't been able to convince employers to hire or promote you, perhaps you and others you know with complementary skills can create an entrepreneurial opportunity and turn an unmet need or passion into a business enterprise.

People of all ages need to have services performed for them that they can no longer do, don't have the time to do, don't know how to do, or simply don't want to do, and are willing to pay someone to handle these tasks for them.

Out-of-work attorneys and social workers can become advocates for patients and persons with disabilities. Unemployed contractors, accountants, and public relations people together can create a

Your employment journey

business that publicizes their work to modify kitchens, bathrooms, and bedrooms for individuals whose physical circumstances have changed.

Whatever path you take, if possible, keep the income stream after (or if) you secure full-time work. Everyone can use extra cash, and job security is nonexistent for some and a distant memory for others. Better safe than sorry.

26 Understand that, generally, it's your employer's party and you're an invited guest.

Traditionally, American employers have the right to discharge employees with or without a good reason. In this situation, individuals are employed at will.

The "at-will" category encompasses employees who are not protected by express employment contracts that state they may be fired only for good cause.

"Good cause" requirements are typically outlined in an individual's employment agreement (usually an executive) or in collective bargaining agreements negotiated by employee unions; nonunion workers rarely have this form of protection. The at-will doctrine also does not apply to contracts for a specified term, such as an employment contract that contemplates the employee serving for an expressly designated number of years.

No matter what anyone tells you, usually it's your employer's party and you are merely an invited guest, but there is good news and bad news.

The bad news is that, absent extenuating circumstances (often legal), your employer may discharge you at any time. The good news is that you can resign at any time, although it is customary to give two weeks' notice. You also have rights you can assert if your discharge violates one of many laws.

27 Don't let it happen; make it happen.

You must be an engaged, active participant in your job search and career-development efforts after you find a job. It's up to you to do what needs to be done to be successful, as you define success. Don't give up or give in unless and until you give it your best. Your future depends on you.

SECTION II

Logistics & Self-Awareness

CHAPTER THREE

Eye of the Tiger

*Nothing in the world can take the place of Persistence.
Talent will not; nothing is more common than unsuccessful
men with talent. Genius will not; unrewarded genius is
almost a proverb. Education will not; the world is full of
educated derelicts. Persistence and determination alone
are omnipotent. The slogan "Press On" has solved and
always will solve the problems of the human race.*

—Calvin Coolidge, thirtieth President
of the United States of America

28 Understand, accept, and brace yourself
for a drain on your energy.

29 Realize that you have a limited amount of energy
and time to devote to the number of tasks you
have to fit into a twenty-four-hour day.

30 Get into the right state of mind and remain focused.

31 Train like an athlete because you'll need endurance
and strength on your employment journey.

The search for employment and on-the-job success in a highly competitive job market requires that you prepare yourself mentally, physically, and emotionally. You may have financial problems, suffer rejection, fail to receive responses or acknowledgements to résumés and telephone calls, and be ignored at work. Don't be embarrassed to acknowledge how you feel and do something about it.

The Holistic Root to Managing Anxiety by Maria Tabone is just one available resource that offers a number of options for managing the stress and anxiety you will likely experience on your journey to employment success. Additional resources are provided at the end of this chapter, and in the Career Toolkit at the end of the book.

As you begin, compare yourself to athletes who prepare for the Olympics by training strenuously for long hours over many years. Achieving Olympic gold undeniably requires single-minded focus and unwavering commitment.

To be successful, Olympic athletes are willing to sacrifice and train for many hours over many days, months, and years to condition themselves to compete in the Olympics. Although there is no guarantee that their hard work will bring them Olympic medals, they nonetheless put in the time and the effort because even the possibility that they will win a medal is worth the sacrifices they make.

Whether you're looking for employment or are fortunate enough to already have a job, success in either situation requires mental and physical readiness to prepare you for the emotional rollercoaster that now accompanies looking for a job or keeping the job you have.

32 Motivate yourself.

*Imagination is the beginning of creation. You
imagine what you desire, you will what you
imagine, and at last you create what you will.*

—George Bernard Shaw, Irish playwright and
cofounder of the London School of Economics

When the world says, "Give up," Hope
whispers, "Try it one more time."

—Author unknown

Take a picture of a resort where you want to vacation; the motorcy-cle, car, or home you would love to buy; or some other item that you dream of owning one day. If you want to be a business executive, find a picture of an executive office in a magazine. If a job is what your dreams are made of, or you see it as a means to acquire the things you want to do or purchase, find a picture that captures your vision of the ideal job.

Next, place the picture in a beautiful frame that pleases your eye, and tape unframed copies on your mirrors and on your refrigerator. If you're employed, place the framed picture on your desk at work; if you're unemployed, place it next to your bed so it is the last image you see before you go to sleep. Every time you get upset about your job or discouraged because you've been unable to find work, look at the picture and try harder.

Tell yourself, "I can achieve anything that I put my mind and my best efforts toward achieving." After you tell yourself that you can do anything, and you set out to achieve your goal, don't let anyone tell you that you can't or shouldn't.

Keep in mind that success means different things to different people. For example:

- If you want to be a plumber, learn from experienced plumbers to be the best plumber you can be.

- If you want to be an executive, research what other successful executives have done to arrive at the position you want to achieve.

If you reasonably believe that you and your contribution are exem-plary, don't let anyone marginalize them. Executives who have been labeled A, B, and C players in one company have gone on to achieve

Motivate yourself.

huge success as A players in much more successful, respected, and highly regarded companies. If your supervisor hasn't told you how you're doing, ask him or her.

Family and friends are a different matter. Depending on the quality of your personal and professional support network, you may need to marshal the strength to repel and distance yourself from your detractors if they're members of your family. If they are "friends," find new ones.

Don't be swayed by what others think and believe is important unless you respect their opinions. Even then, gather more data. Contact others whose opinions you respect, such as a former teacher, coach, professor, supervisor, superior officer, or anyone who has demonstrated sound judgment. Ask them what they think about your goals, given what they know about you.

The person whose opinion you seek should either have specific or generic experience in the business or profession of interest to you, or be someone who can obtain feedback for you from someone who does.

If the gathered data support the conclusion that you're average or not likely to be successful in the role you envision for yourself, consider whether to redirect your efforts. If you feel strongly and passionately about your career selection, don't give up your dreams and goals.

33 Stay in shape or get in shape. (Consult a physician before you begin any fitness program.)

Whatever your employment situation, your physical well-being is critical to your success in finding a job and as an employee. You may find that you have more energy at the end of the day if you begin it with physical activity, such as cycling or walking.

In addition to exercise, balanced meals and healthy eating may also keep your mind sharp and your body in shape, and give you the staying power you need to get the job done.

Daily meditation can relieve stress and anxiety by clearing your head and placing you in a state of mind that permits you to concentrate on your job search or earn a promotion. If you don't care for gyms or can't afford to join one, search the Internet for free online exercise videos, join a neighborhood community center, or borrow exercise DVDs from the library or purchase one. Make an effort to set aside a minimum of one hour each morning for some type of exercise, including strength training.

Try to go to a local track for a walk or jog. Don't let inclement weather sidetrack your fitness efforts. Exercise DVDs are a convenient, inexpensive alternative to running or walking outdoors. Additional sources may be found in the Career Toolkit at the end of the book.

Weight is a sensitive subject but one that should be addressed. Personal struggles aside, you don't have to be a lean, mean employment machine, but you should know that being overweight can affect your employment success. It's no secret that being overweight contributes to medical issues. It's also common knowledge that healthcare premiums (some of which may be paid by employers) are expensive, and there is no sign that they're going to get cheaper.

If you don't have health issues and you're satisfied with how you look, don't change unless that is what you want to do. Be mindful, however, that physical appearance is more important in some industries than in others. Fashion and retail, client-facing sales, and on-air television roles are just a few industries and positions where preference and attention are given to appearance.

If you decide to trim down, find a workout partner to join you in your fitness routine. It's easier to maintain a program if you have someone to exercise with you or keep you company. Make sure your partner is reliable and committed to achieving results. You could also create a networking opportunity through the people you meet on the track or at the gym.

34 | Take a break ... be kind to yourself!

Even Olympic athletes take a break from their intense training schedules, and you should, too. It's unhealthy to maintain a frenetic pace for extended periods of time without a break. Do something you can afford to do without feeling guilty. It'll defeat the purpose if you splurge when you can't afford it. For example:

- Take a day off.

- Go to the movies or a play, or get a manicure earlier in the week when prices may be lower.

- Do something that has nothing to do with your employment efforts.

- Try not to think about what you need to do the following day.

Be kind to yourself because, if you've worked as hard as you should, you'll not only deserve the break, you'll need it.

Don't get it twisted: You need to take a break periodically to avoid or minimize the undesirable stress and anxiety that you'll experience as you search for a job, especially if you've been looking for a long time or you're unhappy with the job you have.

You may be tempted, but please don't resort to alcohol or anything else that will dull your senses and adversely affect your ability to do what is necessary to be successful.

You need to be ready, not hung over, when opportunity knocks or phones. Also plan to avoid anything that will compromise your ability to be alert, make good decisions, and work toward your goal of an eight-hour workday.

35 Don't give up or give in.

If your lack of success in finding a job or receiving a promotion makes you feel underappreciated by prospective employers or ignored by your supervisor despite your marketable skills, conduct a reality check.

Ask yourself:

- Have I exhausted all possible avenues that could lead me to success?

- Have I been more flexible than I've ever been?

- Have I stepped outside of my comfort zone?

- Have I engaged in introspective reflection to identify areas that may need improvement?

Even if you're satisfied that the answers to all these questions are "yes," and you believe that you're close to success, you're likely to realize that this journey you're now on can be humbling.

Don't give up or give in to your emotional ups and downs. Stay the course ... press on. Failure (at least on a permanent basis) isn't an option.

Prepare for Your Job Search Journey

BOOKS

Maria Tabone, *The Holistic Root to Managing Anxiety,* provides a number of options for managing the stress and anxiety you will likely experience as you look for employment. http://www.amazon.com/The-Holistic-Root-Managing-Anxiety/dp/0615356222

Al Siebert, *The Resiliency Advantage: Master Change, Thrive Under Pressure, and Bounce Back from Setbacks,* helps readers banish negative, self-defeating thoughts and improves problem-solving skills. http://www.amazon.com/The-Resiliency-Advantage-Pressure-Setbacks/dp/1576753298

Richard N. Bolles, *What Color is Your Parachute?,* is considered by many to be the seminal job search/career resource. http://www.amazon.com/What-Color-Your-Parachute-2013/dp/1607741474

WEBSITES

http://www.theholisticroot.com

http://www.oflikeminds.com/Unemployment.html

http://www.theladders.com/career-advice/hot-topics/anxiety-depression-job-search

http://ezinearticles.com/?Unemployed?-Tips-To-Go-From-Being-Unemployed-To-Employed&id=117695

http://suite101.com/article/unemployment-job-loss-advice-a33739

http://careerspeed.com/articles/managing_finances_unemployed

http://exercise.about.com/od/healthinjuries/a/olympictraining.htm

http://www.cvtips.com/career_advice_forum/entries/489-Five-tips-for-job-hunting

http://www.foxbusiness.com/personal-finance/2011/09/27/five-job-hunting-tips-for-recent-grads

http://www.huffingtonpost.com/2012/01/04/what-advice-do-you-have-for-job-searchers_n_1182015.html

CHAPTER FOUR

Networking Is the GPS to Employment Success®

Reveal not every secret you have to a friend, for how can you tell but that friend may hereafter become an enemy. And bring not all mischief you are able to upon an enemy, for he may one day become your friend.

—Saadi Shirazi, poet (1184–1291)

SOCIAL WHAT?

Social media is a great tool. By all means, use Facebook and Twitter, as well as texting and any other means of communication that connects you with people and allows you to tell them that you need their help to find a job. Your use, however, should not be detrimental to your efforts to secure employment.

C. COPYRIGHT 2012 PARTHENON ENTERPRISES INC.   Artwork by LYMAN DALLY

36   Use social media wisely.

It's no secret that some employers use social media to screen prospective employees. Friends and other contacts may search for you on Google or look you up on Facebook or LinkedIn before they refer you. Consequently, you want to make sure that you don't have anything on social media sites that hampers your efforts to find a job.

All job-search materials you post on social networks of any kind must be accurate, be consistent with similar materials found elsewhere, and convey a level of professionalism. If the material you've posted is controversial, unflattering, or doesn't otherwise meet these requirements, remove the material from your social-networking sites.

LinkedIn: LinkedIn is primarily a business site used by recruiters and job seekers. It's a place to look up people and companies by name, geographical area, and location or college. Always keep your profile updated so recruiters and former colleagues can connect with you.

If you decide to create a LinkedIn profile, be careful. Your LinkedIn profile is (or should be) a short version of your résumé. Make sure the two are consistent.

LinkedIn is a tool you may use in several different ways:

■   To get your information to recruiters who will search the www.linkedin.com database; and

- For you to look up information about the people who will interview you.

For example, if you know that you will be interviewing with Jane Doe of the ABC Company, you can look up Jane Doe on LinkedIn, and then look at whatever Jane has chosen to post about herself. It may be a short bio or a synopsis of work experience and education.

Social media sites like LinkedIn are great tools to find out about the people you're going to meet, what is going on in the company, and connect with colleagues and contacts. You can reach out and establish a connection, which may lead to connections with people through a second or third source.

Whatever you do, make sure that your digital footprint is scrubbed. Monitor it regularly to be sure it remains that way. Don't post inappropriate statuses or pictures under any circumstances, particularly if you're friends with coworkers.

- Even though there is an understood line between work life and personal life, don't assume it's normal to share everything with coworkers.

- Revise your settings accordingly if you're friends with coworkers and want a certain level of privacy.

- Keep in mind that passwords and privacy settings don't always work effectively.

37 Don't engage in conduct that you wouldn't want your loved ones to view in any form of media, including social-networking sites.

Not long ago, examples of career-limiting or inappropriate behavior included:

- Unprofessional, rude, or obscene conduct

- Drunkenness

- Disorderly or criminal activity on the job or in public

The rule of thumb is, "Don't do anything you wouldn't want to read about on the front page of *The New York Times* or *The Wall Street Journal*," after which your loved ones would ask, "What were you thinking?" In other words, don't embarrass yourself or the people important to you. Technology changed that standard, just as it's contributed to the change in the entire employment landscape.

Social networking: To paraphrase Merriam-Webster, networking is the exchange of information, data, or services among people as individuals or in groups or institutions, particularly to cultivate and further productive employment or business relationships.

The Social Networking website defines social networking as:

> … [T]he grouping of individuals into specific groups, like small rural communities or a neighborhood subdivision, if you will. Although social networking is possible in person, especially in the workplace, universities, and high schools, it is most popular online. This is because unlike most high schools, colleges, or workplaces, the Internet is filled with millions of individuals who are looking to meet other people, to gather and share first-hand information and experiences about any number of topics … from golfing, gardening, developing friendships and professional alliances.[6]

Significantly, the foregoing definitions include references to "employment," "business," and "workplace." By some accounts, approximately 30 percent of employers use Facebook to screen prospective employees. Think about that before you post sexually explicit, provocative pictures or exchanges that contain inappropriate or questionable language, references, or statements that may come back to haunt you.

"Tell-All Generation Learns to Keep Things Offline"[7] is an article that everyone should read, not just members of the Tell-All Generation. The article speaks to anyone who is social-network obsessed and texts, posts, and tweets without an eye to the future.

Issues of privacy aside, "[s]ocial networking requires vigilance, not only in what you post, but what your friends post about you."[8] The article describes individuals under thirty who began sharing their lives and opinions on social networks as teenagers,but who, as adults, wish they had censored themselves more and shared less.

In truth, adults are as addicted to Facebook and other social media sites as the Tell-All Generation. The ease with which information can be shared with "friends" and loved ones, including highlights of family events, permits people to connect and remain connected whether they're near or far away.

If you don't know what conduct is inappropriate or questionable, ask yourself, "If this behavior was pictured or described in the newspaper or on the nightly newscast, would my grandmother be embarrassed?"

38 | Consider the possible long-term consequences before you post material on social-networking sites.

If you're young and your entire life lies ahead, you may think that you can do whatever you want now. Think again. Picture the facial expression on the person who was about to offer you the job of your dreams and become your boss, or your current boss who was considering you for promotion, when he or she sees your spring-break photos or the "love" video you and the person you thought you were going to marry posted on a social network.

Yahoo Finance identifies the following as the "6 Career-Killing Facebook Mistakes":

1. Inappropriate pictures;

2. Complaining about your current job;

3. Posting information that conflicts with your résumé;

4. Statuses you wouldn't want your boss to see;

5. Not understanding your security settings; and

6. Losing by association.[9]

A thorough review of the article is worthwhile. Posting provocative material that may adversely affect or limit your employment opportunities may have other unintended consequences. Transmitting sexually graphic pictures of underage individuals, even with their consent, may violate child pornography laws, which could lead to criminal prosecution.

|39| If you "friend" a coworker, be sure not to post anything that might be used against you to damage your reputation at work.

Current friends with access to your page or site may inadvertently or jokingly disclose sensitive material, or in the future become "frenemies" or even outright enemies. As you know, romances and friendships do not always end on amicable terms. Making sound decisions now will allow you to maintain more options in the future.

A picture is worth a thousand words: Sexting, love-making films, and vacation frivolity—such as baring it all in front of a camera—may seem harmless, especially if your judgment is impaired by alcohol, drugs, or medication, but there are risks.

■   Please proceed with caution.

■   Be discreet.

■   What you do behind closed doors is your business, but it's risky to record or otherwise preserve private, especially sexually explicit, photos.

Consider this scenario:

☑ Theresa complained that June, her supervisor, didn't like her because she is an atheist, and that June induced a coworker named Albert, who also reported to June, to sexually harass Theresa. Her employer initiated an internal investigation to determine whether Theresa's allegations had merit.

To prove her allegation of sexual harassment, Theresa produced a sexually graphic picture of Albert that he had sexted her. When Albert was questioned, he laughed. He said, among other things, that he and Theresa had a consensual sexual relationship, and he could prove it. Albert forwarded a nude picture of Theresa that she had sent him.

Theresa was discharged because she'd filed a bogus complaint. That is but one lesson. Imagine how you would feel if intimate pictures of you were circulated in the workplace, even on a limited basis.

Privacy ... technology: Technology has revolutionized social networking. Don't forget, however, that electronic and paper record trails can follow you indefinitely. The commonly held belief that information, communications, and pictures posted on social networks and transmitted by computers, cell phones, and other technology are accessible only to individuals selected and approved by the page owner is simply incorrect.

- Review your page often, even daily, while you're searching for employment.

- You may be judged by the company you keep, as indicated by the material on your page.

It's up to you to make sure that any material, such as provocative pictures and language from "friends," which cast you in an unfavorable light, are removed from your page before they can do any harm to your efforts to find a job.

Twitter: Tweeting after an interview, boasting about how awesomely you performed, and including negative comments about the interviewers, or calling into question their intellect because they bought your "act" or you "got one over on them," is a bad idea. If somehow an interviewer sees the tweet, you can kiss your dream position goodbye. Likewise, derogatory or otherwise uncomplimentary tweets about your employer, supervisor, or coworkers can have a career-limiting effect.

Whether you're employed or seeking employment, imagine that, down the road and years from now, you become a parent, and you're being considered for a high-level position with a company, or the President of the United States offers you a cabinet post. What will you say to your loved ones, particularly your children, when the forgotten films of your youth are shown?

To avoid the experience, you should forego immediate gratification and the knee-jerk temptation to communicate and otherwise share the first thought that comes to mind as well as controversial pictures you wouldn't want shared with the world.

Ask yourself, "Is it worth it?"

Let me answer for you: "No!"

You may be entitled to privacy, but your privacy is not guaranteed. Furthermore, social networks may start out with strong privacy policies but may change over time for financial reasons.

If you're not sure you're making the right decision, ask someone whose opinion you respect because he or she has a proven record of staying out of trouble and moving ahead at work, and a reputation for doing well in life given his or her age, education, and experience.

To summarize, early in life you may not consider your conduct indiscreet and inappropriate; later in life, you probably will.

- Workplace relationships that go bad, such as a friendship or a love affair, can have career-limiting consequences.

- "Live" inappropriate behavior and sexually graphic or otherwise provocative pictures and communications posted on social networks should be avoided at all costs.

Social Media/Networking

http://blogs.findlaw.com/official_findlaw_blog/2013/06/tips-for-managing-your-career-on-social-media.html

http://company.findlaw.com/press-center/2013/tips-for-managing-your-career-on-social-media.html

http://www.fox54.com/story/22398844/tips-for-managing-your-career-on-social-media

http://www.forbes.com/sites/susanadams/2011/06/07/networking-is-still-the-best-way-to-find-a-job-survey-says/

http://company.findlaw.com/press-center/2013/tips-for-managing-your-career-on-social-media.html

http://www.cvtips.com/career_advice_forum/entries/501-Conducting-a-Job-Search-With-New-Technology-The-Benefits-of-Social-Media

http://finance.yahoo.com/news/pf_article_109267.html

http://jobsearch.about.com/cs/networking/a/networking.htm

http://www.bankrate.com/finance/personal-finance/5-networking-strategies-to-a-new-job-2.aspx

Network, network, network, network

(Old-School and New-School) Networking

40 It's a high-tech world, but don't forget the human factor.

41 Tell everyone you know, and anyone you meet but don't know, that you're looking for a job and you need their help.

Many, if not most, people get jobs through networking. There are great stories about people getting job leads from unexpected places. The second story below is not technically networking but rather the result of a candidate's powerful interview and the positive impression she made on a prospective employer.

☑ Two coworkers, who were employed as compensation professionals at an energy company, were miserable in their jobs. They had joined the company around the same time, and both lamented their decision to accept positions with the company. One of the workers couldn't take it any longer and resigned after eighteen months, leaving his colleague behind, but they kept in touch.

One day, the employee who was left behind received a call from another employer, inviting her to come for an interview. At first, she didn't understand because she had not applied for a job with this company. To her surprise, she found out that she had been referred by her former colleague, who had been offered the job but turned it down. Within four weeks of her first interview, she received a job offer, which she happily accepted.

☑ A woman applied for a position with a prominent pharmaceutical company. The interview with the manager went extremely well, so the candidate was very disappointed when the manager informed her that she hadn't been selected for the position. This highly regarded company would have represented a significant coup for future employment opportunities if she could include it on her résumé. The manager asked her, however, if she would consider another position if one became available. Of course, the candidate said yes.

About five or six weeks later, the former candidate received a call from the manager. She was excited to think that another opportunity with the pharmaceutical company had become available. Although she hoped to receive a job offer, she was somewhat leery that there was another vacancy within the department so soon.

As it turned out, the manager was calling to offer her a position not at the pharmaceutical company but at the corporate headquarters of a much larger, global organization. The manager had left the pharmaceutical company but remembered the former candidate.

They met for lunch after her call, during which the manager described the job and told the woman that the position, should she choose to accept it, was hers.

These scenarios illustrate the importance of being the person that a former coworker would recommend for a job that he turned down, and being so impressive during an interview that the interviewer remembers you favorably and offers to hire you at a later date. If you make a commitment to do the work necessary, you can become the person others think of when they're asked if they know anyone they can recommend.

One way to maximize the likelihood that favorable job-search results will be achieved is to embrace both old-school and new-school networking. Both methods should be used simultaneously and vigorously to achieve employment success. To use an old-school phrase, "Leave no stone unturned."

The new-school approach to almost everything in this high-tech world is to rely on social networking for everything, from looking for a job to communicating thoughts, ideas, hopes, and dreams.

If you're new school:

- You may feel that you should have a job simply because you graduated from college, or simply because you want or need one; and

- You focus primarily (if not exclusively) on Internet-based job boards for employment opportunities.

If you have this mindset, you'll be surprised when you're not contacted for an interview, especially when you've followed up and followed up and followed up.

Apparently, you didn't get the text message or e-mail, which informed you that in this new-school, high-tech, electronic world, there is simply no substitute for old-school, "live," person-to-person contact. This method of networking, especially through referrals and recommendations, can almost magically get a person in the door for at least an exploratory or courtesy interview.

The reasons are simple. Given the number of talented, educated, skilled people who are looking for work, hiring decisions made in the worst economy since the Great Depression will be based in part on intangibles.

These decisions will also be driven by first impressions based on personal appearance and ability to communicate, as well as:

- Who knows whom;

- Who referred whom;

- Who is related to whom;

- Who owes whom a favor; and

- Who wants to get in good with the person who made the referral.

The goal is to include all possible strategies and advantages in your job-search arsenal. You may be surprised by the number of people you know and how extensive your networks are when you tap into them. You're probably already networking without knowing it.

To expand your network, you shouldn't hesitate to talk to everyone you know and everyone you meet: friends, family, your dry cleaner, people in restaurants, strangers on trains and planes, people where you worship, and anywhere else. Cast a wide net.

☑ John was employed by a midsized company as Director of Staff Development. One Friday afternoon, his supervisor Hector, the Vice President of Human Resources, simply walked into John's office and told him that the company they worked for had just lost two of its biggest clients. Projected cost-cutting measures included the elimination of John's division and the layoffs of John and the four people he supervised. John was out of a job. Unfortunately, he hadn't seen it coming, so he wasn't prepared.

Later that Friday evening, John and his girlfriend Ming went to dinner at the local pizza parlor, which was owned by the family of John's best friend Troy. Troy, who was working that evening, came over to John and Ming's table to say hi and to ask John if he wanted to watch the football game together on Sunday.

With one look at John's face, Troy immediately realized that something was very wrong. He hesitated to intrude but was concerned, so he asked, "Hey, bro. Is everything okay? You look like someone died."

John, who was a proud, young man, wasn't in the mood to share his bad news. Troy was his best friend, but John was embarrassed. Ming gave him a look and said, "You might as well tell him. He'll find out eventually."

When Troy heard that John had lost his job, he said, "I may know someone who can help."

Lee Turner, one of the pizza parlor's frequent lunch customers, had been in that afternoon, and Troy had overheard him say to his colleague that he was looking for a training consultant. Troy tactfully connected Lee and John. The connection led to a temporary assignment for John, which turned into a permanent position at a slightly higher salary than John had made previously.

You'll be amazed that even strangers will be willing to help. So often, people—many of them women—go through life helping others but forget to ask for help for themselves. Never be afraid or too proud to ask for help. Tell people that you're looking for employment and what your skills and background are. Give or send them your résumé. If possible, meet them for coffee, dressed to send the message that they won't regret taking the time to meet with you.

Of course, remember that they aren't obligated to you, and they have a choice. You want them to choose to help you, and be glad—even proud—that they did.

☑ While waiting in the checkout line at the grocery store, Sela, a soft-spoken, mild-mannered young woman, overheard a conversation between a woman behind her named Molly and another woman in line.

Molly said that she conducted career-advice workshops for a local civic association. Sela waited for Molly outside the store, told her that she was looking for a job, and asked for her help.

After Sela described her efforts to find a job and her frustration—in her words, "No one will help me"—Molly agreed to review her résumé. She remembered that she had begun to offer the workshops to help people with their job searches.

Molly saw the problem right away: Sela's résumé didn't showcase her skills. She had merely listed her work experience and described her responsibilities generically. There was no "oomph" in her descriptions of her extensive employment history.

For example, Sela said that she worked on a project with coworkers. After listening to her explanation of her role on the project, Molly changed it to "contributed substantially to the success of a departmental initiative that improved productivity by 20 percent." Employers love measurable results that demonstrate improvement.

Molly reworked the résumé, sent it to Sela, and awaited her response. It came as a pleasant surprise to Molly to learn that the changes she had made to Sela's résumé worked immediately.

Sela contacted Molly with great news: She had received a telephone interview! Again, she asked for Molly's help. This time, Molly directed Sela to material on how to prepare for telephone and in-person interviews found on the www.youremploymentmatters.com website.

Sela read the material, followed the recommendations, "practiced, practiced, and practiced," and landed a "live," in-person interview. She put on her interview outfit, sat in front of a mirror to see how she looked sitting down, and made adjustments in her outfit to achieve the look she desired. Sela also practiced answering interview questions in front of her mirror.

She nailed it! Sela told Molly that she had applied for an entry-level position but, because of her considerable experience, her education, and her interview performance, she was offered a higher position.

Although Sela attributed her success to Molly's contribution, Molly knew better. Sela was successful because she stepped outside her comfort zone and asked a stranger for help. As intelligent, educated, and otherwise talented as Sela is, she simply didn't know how to position herself to achieve successful job search results.

PREPARATION

Adopt the Boy Scout motto—"Be Prepared"—by planning what you'll say during a networking opportunity and practicing how you'll say it.

First: Prepare a ninety-second marketing pitch that is a personal, self-serving commercial about YOU. It's an opportunity to highlight your attributes, such as verbal and written skills, technical skills, poise, presence, and personality.

Your marketing pitch should include the following key points:

- Your experience, strengths, accomplishments

- The type of work or position you're seeking

- Why you are interested in that type of work or industry

- Why you're attending the event or what you're seeking (optional)

You should allocate the ninety seconds as follows:

- A brief statement about your education (fifteen seconds)

- Your early work experience and key accomplishments (twenty seconds)

- Your most recent experiences and key achievements (twenty-five seconds)

- What you can do for an employer and what you have to offer, including soft skills and your future focus (thirty seconds)

For many, if not most, positions, soft skills—such as problem solving and analytical ability—and a positive attitude are as important to employers as education, employment experience, and technical proficiency.

Feel free to reallocate the ninety seconds if your work experience or education is particularly interesting or impressive. Keep in mind that people value their time and may not be willing to listen to lengthy soliloquies. Make it short, interesting, and memorable, and deliver it crisply.

After a concise, informative marketing pitch is drafted, the next thing to do is practice, practice, practice. The objective is to achieve a smooth, polished delivery in ninety seconds that exudes confidence, competence, and professionalism.

Make no mistake: It takes time to draft and master an effective marketing pitch, but it's an invaluable tool that will be useful after you find employment.

☑ Christine, a former executive, attended a reception hosted by the alumni of a local university's business school. The well-attended event was held at a lovely venue with several large rooms and comfortable outside seating. It was an ideal networking opportunity.

Recent business school graduates Beth, Alexandra, and Jerry were introduced to attendees by professors or staff members. Each young person was poised, pleasant, and engaged. Everyone exchanged business cards.

After a discussion about the changes in the employment landscape and what young people needed to do to increase their employment opportunities, Christine said her goodbyes and left the reception to have dinner with friends in the main dining room.

Before she was seated, Jerry walked up to her with his hand extended and reintroduced himself.

"Hello again, Ms. Bryant. I'm Jerry Charles. I met you inside at the reception. I just graduated with an MBA in marketing. I'm working at Global Company as an intern. I hope I'll get hired in a full-time position but, if I don't, I'm looking for a position with a company that can use my technical and marketing skills."

Christine was floored. It was as if Jerry had attended one of her career-readiness workshops. He understood that he had a limited amount of time to convey his message and pitch himself (as his product) persuasively and make a favorable impression. Jerry had nailed the marketing pitch.

Christine agreed to help Jerry with his efforts to find a job. When Jerry returned from vacation, she wasn't surprised to learn that her help wasn't needed. Jerry had been offered a position with a Fortune 500 company, which he accepted.

You may notice that Jerry's pitch was short and didn't cover his early work experience and key accomplishments. What Jerry delivered in a very limited amount of time was impressive and compelling. His professional appearance and demeanor, posture, firm handshake, and flawlessly delivered pitch sealed the deal for Christine. Jerry made her want to help him find a job.

Second: Mastering the social graces is another old-school approach that yields positive results. There is an opportunity to be viewed favorably during your job search by:

- Smiling;

- Holding doors open;

- Saying "please" and "thank you" to everyone who provides assistance (even in a small way);

- Listening intently; and

- Making eye contact.

If someone is especially kind or encouraging before or after an interview, find out the person's name and send the person a thank-you note. Even better, make an effort to find the individual after the interview to thank him or her in person. He will remember you favorably. If an employment opportunity arises, you may be the person she thinks of to assume the role because you left a positive impression.

An expression of your appreciation that you may consider an insignificant gesture and simply being polite may cause someone to conclude that you're the kind of person he wants to work with each day.

Thank-you notes should always be sent to contacts who have helped you and anyone who interviewed you individually or in a group. Your failure to do so may be considered a lack of interest or a glaring omission that will be held against you.

Caution: Don't assume that older individuals aren't technically savvy. Many of them have wholeheartedly embraced new-school approaches to communication. Use your powers of observation and knowledge about the person to determine whether to use e-mail or snail mail to thank those with whom you have met or those who have helped you.

Third: Old-school familiarity with the rules of etiquette is also essential. You don't want to give anyone the impression that you're not ready for prime time because you put your napkin under your chin at a business dinner, or picked your teeth with your fingernail because that kernel of corn was driving you crazy. The purchase of

Emily Post's Etiquette, 18th ed.[10] in hardcover or paperback, which is a comprehensive, modern guide to managing yourself in polite society, may be in order. There is also a series of books called *Gentle Manners*, which are easy-to-carry, quick references for social situations. Titles include:

- *How to Be a Gentleman Revised & Updated: A Contemporary Guide to Common Courtesy (GentleManners)*[11]

- *How to Be a Lady Revised & Updated: A Contemporary Guide to Common Courtesy (GentleManners)*[12]

- *As a Gentleman Would Say: Responses to Life's Important (and Sometimes Awkward) Situations (GentleManners)*[13]

- *As a Lady Would Say Revised & Updated: Responses to Life's Important (and Sometimes Awkward) Situations (GentleManners)*[14]

If your public library does not have them, ask the librarian to consider ordering them, or ask for any of them as a gift. Present yourself so there is no question that you are better suited than anyone else to represent the company as an employee.

Now you're ready for networking—old-school and new-school style: It may be difficult to believe, but there are so many ways people can help you, and they're usually willing. They simply may not think of how they can be helpful.

Make a list of the people you know and contact them all to tell them that you need a job. Tell them that you'd like their help. It's up to you to identify how they can help.

Ask them if they can introduce you to other people who will introduce you to other people. Someone may be an HR person who can review your résumé and give you feedback. Someone may know someone else who has an open position. It's important to be specific about the type of position you seek.

Tell them you'll call them to follow up, and do so two weeks later if you haven't heard from the person. Understand, however, that finding a job for you is higher on your "to-do" list than it is on the other person's list. It's important to give people time to contact others on your behalf.

You have to follow up persistently, but politely. You simply can't afford to rely on anyone else to care as much about getting you employed as you do. You have to own your job search and manage it. If you sit back and wait for an e-mail or telephone call that may never come, you will likely be out of work for a very long time.

Ask them whether they have any advice for you, whether there is anyone they know who can give you a lead or give you advice, and to think about any possible opportunities no matter how indefinite. Be sure to write down everything and follow up.

Attend professional, community, and political events as networking activities where you meet people you know and people you don't know.

- Try to obtain the names of expected speakers and attendees in advance, so you can research them and connect with as many of them as possible.

- If you meet someone you admire, or someone whose job you want to have one day, ask them lots of questions, such as:

  - "How did you achieve your goals?" (People love to talk about themselves.)

  - "What challenges did you face along the way?"

  - "What do you love about your job?"

  - What do you not like about your job?"

- The mastery of your marketing pitch will help you engage people in conversation.

As you network, it's helpful to create a "win-win" situation by doing something that benefits the other person. For example, suppose one of your friends has an uncle who is an HR director at a company headquartered in the next town. You have a cousin who works for an advertising agency that represents the NFL. Your cousin can get tickets to almost any NFL game, if the game isn't sold out.

Before you make the offer to your friend, make sure your cousin can get the tickets. If your cousin can't help you out, ask the friend to introduce you to the uncle anyway. What have you got to lose?

You have nothing to lose by identifying the people in your extended network and contacting them. Use your networks. Keep talking to people. They'll tell you to call two friends and you'll call them, and then they'll tell you to call two more friends, and so on.

Looking for a job takes time and a lot of hard work for which there is no substitute. The possibilities are endless, but it takes time, patience, and perseverance. First and foremost, people must know that you need and want help. To be sure that they know, you have to tell them. Please don't leave it to anyone else.

It's your future. *Own it!*

- Use and expand your networks by continuing to talk to people "live" and through social media.

- Do not let pride get in the way.

- Introduce yourself to people you don't know, and tell them that you're looking for work.

- Yes, you can talk to strangers. You're an adult on a mission.

- Don't succumb to fears and insecurities.

- Take a deep breath and step outside your comfort zone.

- If you don't think someone will be helpful, don't let that prevent you from connecting with the person. If nothing else, you'll have a new contact to add to your network database.

- The goal is to establish a vast network that will help you find a job.

After securing employment, your network should be maintained. You'll find it useful in the future.

It isn't unusual to lose data and contacts on smartphones, cell phones, and other electronic devices. It's inexcusable to miss an opportunity that could have led to a job because you failed to secure essential data.

As you network:

- Be sure to create a database.

- Back up the database on an external hard drive.

- All contacts (old and new), with names, e-mail, and home or business addresses and various telephone numbers, should be added to your electronic database and backed up.

Don't get it twisted: One more time—use social media, but use it wisely.

The new-school approach, which favors the speed of more impersonal electronic submissions and social networks to share information and communicate thoughts, ideas, hopes, and dreams, is a critical element of your networking strategy.

Unquestionably, electronic tablets, laptops, smartphones, and various types of social media are useful tools and essential to achieving employment success, especially in a recessionary economy; however, it's foolhardy to rely on them exclusively or even primarily.

There was a time when people who wanted to work could find a job. As anyone who is currently looking for employment knows, times have changed. Nonetheless, the use of both old-school and new-school approaches to express yourself and your skills effectively and consistently as you persistently network is your GPS to Employment Success®.

Networking

http://www.forbes.com/sites/susanadams/2011/06/07/networking-is-still-the-best-way-to-find-a-job-survey-says

http://www.quintcareers.com/tips/career_networking_tips.html

http://career-advice.monster.ca/job-hunt-strategy/professional-networking/jobs.aspx

http://www.enetsc.com/JobSearchTips14.htm

http://www.helpguide.org/life/job_networking_how_to_find_job.htm

http://jobsearch.about.com/od/networking/a/networkingtips.htm

http://money.usnews.com/money/blogs/outside-voices-careers/2011/10/18/6-networking-tips-for-your-job-search

http://www.rileyguide.com/network.html

CHAPTER FIVE

Who Are You?

*You are what you think. You are what
you go for. You are what you do!*

—Bob Richards, athlete

*The best career advice given to the young is: Find out what
you like doing best and get someone to pay you for doing it.*

—Katharine Whitehorn, journalist and author

42 Acknowledge perceptions about your
strengths and weaknesses.

43 By your conduct, refute negative perceptions.

Fairly or unfairly, some people draw conclusions and form judgments
about others without firsthand knowledge or personal experience. If
you were born after 1980, you're a member of Generation Y. If you're
also a recent college graduate with little or no experience, the favorable perceptions about you are that:

- You begin with a clean slate, and you can be trained,
  developed, and molded into the type of employee an
  employer wants;

Artwork by LYMAN DALLY

- You may be eager to take any job, especially one that promises advancement; and

- You have a "sixth sense" that enables you to incorporate technology in all of your personal and global interactions.

Less favorable perceptions might include the idea that you lack experience, which means that you need to be trained. Training takes time and resources. Typically, employers prefer someone who can hit the ground running and function with minimal supervision.

Other, less favorable perceptions are that:

- You may be used to hand-holding and one-on-one attention;

- You may not respect authority;

- You may have unrealistic expectations about your potential;

- You may not accept the concept of teamwork;

- You aren't prepared for work/life realities; and

- You lack focus.

If you're older, the favorable perceptions about you are that:

- You have life experience and a level of maturity;

- You have industry experience and therefore won't require much training;

- You tend to be more reliable than younger people; and

- You are likely to have responsibilities and obligations to others, which make it likely that you need employment.

Less favorable perceptions about older candidates are that:

- You aren't technologically proficient;

- You are resistant to change;

- You aren't eager to learn new things;

- You no longer operate at full speed and aren't fully engaged;

- You rely on your accomplishments of yesterday rather than realize the need to continuously produce at a high level; and

- You think of your job as yours forever.

If you detect somewhat of a contradiction in the favorable and unfavorable perceptions, you're correct. Perceptions depend on the person who has them, their personal experience with and exposure to members of the group, and the last person to whom they spoke who had an opinion.

Whichever group you belong to, you are hired depending on whether the organization or business in which you're interested is willing to invest resources in training inexperienced talent or prefers to select a more seasoned candidate.

INCONVENIENT TRUTHS

Individuals in pursuit of employment will need to be more flexible, creative, and technologically savvy because technological innovation, among other things, has changed the manner in which business is conducted. Relationships are still important, but there has been a shift from doing business face to face through established relationships to handling matters remotely with the emphasis on cost effectiveness.

If you're returning to the workforce after a long absence:

- You might not return to the job level you previously held.

- You might have to do things differently because technology, procedures, and legal considerations have changed.

- You won't know everything, but you can learn.

- You can learn from young people and young people can learn from you. Find a way to make both happen. Ask a young person out to lunch and ask him or her for help. See whether you can make a suggestion that you think might help her or him on a project.

- You may need a makeover.

  - □ For women: Update your makeup, buy new interviewing outfits, and at least get a manicure.

  - □ For men and women: Gray hair adds additional years to your appearance. You need a more youthful look.

Don't get it twisted: Please don't go too far with the youthful look. You don't want to look dowdy or ancient, but dressing too youthfully may cause your judgment to be questioned.

Rather, you want to give off a vibe that communicates energy, confidence, maturity, and a style that is age-appropriate yet youthful. You need to dispel the negative perceptions while you convey that you're a hard worker, a fast learner, willing to take on any job, and the person who should be hired or promoted.

> *Begin somewhere; you cannot build a*
> *reputation on what you intend to do.*

—Liz Smith, gossip columnist and journalist

Your personal brand: Personal branding is a concept that more and more people recognize as an essential element in managing their careers and marketing themselves. Responses to a survey that asked individuals to identify the most important traits of their personal brand, included:

- Verbal communication skills (66 percent)

- Technical knowledge (60 percent)

- Résumés (57 percent)

- Written communications other than résumés (57 percent)

- Personal attire (50 percent)

- Use of social media (35 percent)[15]

Also consider the following definition:

Your personal brand is what other people think of you. In some ways, it's outside your control, but you obviously have some influence over it ...

If you type an e-mail, you're branding yourself. If you have a conversation with a friend or family member, you're branding yourself. How you dress, what you eat, and how you talk all contribute to your brand. Think of your brand as the summation of all the associations about you stored in people's minds.[16]

To summarize, your personal brand is:

- How you present yourself to others;

- Your reputation;

- How people describe you; and

- What people think of you.

Guided by this framework, consider how people who know you will describe your reputation, personal appearance, personality, oral and written communication skills, and social demeanor. At minimum, these elements should form the foundation for your personal brand, which may include seemingly insignificant elements of your individual style and preferences.

As the following story conveys, you may be observed and conclusions may be drawn about you merely because of what you bring with you to a meeting.

☑ Nick, a young manager with executive aspirations, attended many meetings with company executives. It never occurred to him that anyone was paying attention to him during most of these meetings because he was usually along to crunch numbers and provide information to Mahish, his boss, who was the Senior Vice President of Finance.

After one meeting, Rebecca, Vice President of Audit, stopped Nick and said, "I've noticed that you always have a little notebook with you. They're attractive notebooks with different patterns."

Nick was surprised, kept his cool, and replied, "I like a nice notebook, something more than the typical spiral notebook."

Rebecca smiled and responded, "I also like a nice notebook, and so does my husband. Where do you buy yours?"

Thereafter, Nick was on Rebecca's radar screen, which was not a bad place to be. Who would have thought that a notebook would contribute to Nick's effort to distinguish himself at work?

REPUTATION

I f you're just starting out, and you don't have a reputation that precedes you, establish one you can be proud of by conducting yourself with integrity and maturity.

Additionally, whatever your career ambitions are, it's imperative that you're viewed as a professional. Your conduct should reinforce that perception.

The way to gain a good reputation is to endeavor to be what you desire to appear.

—Socrates (ancient Greek philosopher, 470 BC–399 BC)

---

44 Strive to establish a reputation as a person who is hard working, detail oriented, honest, ethical, reliable, punctual, polite, and a team player.

45 View yourself as a professional.

46   By your conduct, create that impression so that others view you likewise.

Your public and private behavior, including what you say, how you say it, and how you present yourself, influence how you are perceived by others. Your reputation evolves over time based on these perceptions and the opinions that result from them.

■ A good reputation takes a long time to build and only moments to destroy.

■ Rehabilitating your reputation is possible, but it also takes a strategic plan and time to execute the plan.

■ A leopard can change its spots, but it takes time and positive experiences to convince skeptics.

■ If your reputation needs improvement, and you're willing to change it:

☐ Be prepared to talk about the changes you've made.

☐ Explain why you have changed.

☐ By your conduct, demonstrate that you are no longer the person you once were.

In the workplace, your reputation may precede you. If it does, you always want it said that you a reliable hard worker, who is creative and resourceful (in other words, someone who thinks outside the box) as well as a person of good character and integrity, who can be relied upon to tell the truth.

Do workers who are dishonest and unfamiliar with the truth prosper? Unfortunately, some of them do, but don't try it. It's not worth the risk.

Before you begin to market yourself in interviews and as you network, find out how self-aware you are by asking:

- "Who am I?"

- "What is my personal brand?"

- "Does my personal brand serve me well or do I need to make changes?"

☑ Mario, a young contestant on one of the popular talent shows, demonstrated a sense of self-awareness that is rare, even in adults. In his interview, which aired as part of the show, Mario said he was in the competition because he needed to know whether or not he was a talented singer.

His parents consistently told Mario how well he sang, but he realized that his parents are biased because they love him. Mario wanted independent, objective affirmation that he had the talent his parents always told him he had.

Unfortunately, Mario didn't win his round, but he won my respect and admiration because he dared to do what many people never even think of. It would have been easier for Mario to believe the positive feedback from his parents, and to believe what he wanted to be true, but Mario courageously sought information, not affirmation.

Like Mario, you need information that will help you be successful rather than affirmation that you're as wonderful as you've been led to believe. (See Tip #6.) As mentioned earlier, ask people who know you and whom you respect—teachers, coaches, neighbors, friends, and clergy—what your strengths and weaknesses are.

You need to find out whether you are:

- An effective communicator;

- A team player;

- Reliable;

- A leader or a person with leadership qualities; or

- A person with special attributes. (If you are, ask them to please list them for you.)

Don't forget to accept feedback as you would a gift: gratefully and graciously. (See Tip #12.) Ask people if they want their feedback to be anonymous. If they do, give them a self-addressed, stamped envelope and ask that they mail their response to you. If they don't require anonymity, they can e-mail their response.

Be sure to send them a written thank-you note. How you send your thank-you depends on what you know about the person. If you know the person is more traditional and might prefer a handwritten note via snail mail, don't send an e-mail. An e-card or e-mail that expresses your appreciation for his or her time and feedback is acceptable if you're sure that the person won't consider it too casual.

47 Embrace differences.

48 Learn from people who are different.

49 Overcome prejudice and biases.

> *We are all different, and should do*
> *what we can do to remain so.*

—Paulo Coelho, lyricist and novelist

Different isn't wrong or inferior; it's simply different. If you go through life avoiding everyone who is not the same as you, you will miss out on a large slice of life and some great experiences.

Regardless of your age or stage in life, you're subject to the vagaries of the inner workings of the employment environment. Consequently, you'll be interacting with others who'll be different from you, have different beliefs, and have different ways of doing things.

Currently, there are four different generations employed in the American workplace:

- Mature/World War II generation (born before 1945)

- Baby Boom generation (born between 1945 and 1964)

- Generation X (born between 1965 and 1979)

- Generation Y/Millennials (born after 1980)

Each generation is influenced by its own defining events and technologies, and has something to offer the team effort. It's counterproductive and rude to be impolite or to summarily dismiss anyone's ideas simply because they're different or they're unfamiliar to you. It may be difficult, but make every effort to disregard pre-existing biases and prejudices.

Consider your coworkers and their differences as an instructional opportunity for you to learn about a variety of cultures, different ways of doing things, and multiple points of view. Likewise, acknowledge the importance of the industry experience and institutional knowledge of employees who are your senior in years of service and work experience. If you have a degree, don't mentally dismiss the contributions of individuals who may not have degrees.

Learn: One of the benefits of working in a multigenerational environment is that there are so many opportunities to learn something new because everyone brings something unique to the discussion. Men and women of different ethnicities, national origins, and religions, regardless of their sexual and gender orientations, gender identities, or disabilities and abilities, all have something to share.

If you're employed, workplace interactions with people who are different include:

- Taking their direction and supervision

- Accepting their solicited and unsolicited feedback, which may be favorable or unfavorable

- Interacting with coworkers, clients, customers, and other third parties who don't even work for your employer

If you're unemployed, interactions include:

- Following directions

- Answering questions

- Waiting for interviews to begin

- Waiting for decisions to be made and for you to be notified of them

Keep in mind that people who don't look or sound like you are people who make decisions about employment matters. These decision makers are looking for people who will contribute to a team and with whom they and other employees would like to work each workday.

50 Avoid discussions about religion, politics, sex, health problems, problems with loved ones, and your career aspirations.

Yes, this is America. Freedom of speech is a fundamental right. Nonetheless, there are topics and viewpoints that may cause people to draw conclusions accurately or inaccurately about your character and intelligence. Religion, politics, sex (particularly your sex life), your health problems, problems with loved ones, and your career aspirations are examples of such topics.

Consequently, there is no advantage to sharing your opinions, your personal practices and situations, and your future-employment aspirations at work with your supervisors and coworkers. These people, who appear to be open-minded and "with it," may instead be less "with it" and more judgmental than you think. More important, you don't want your boss to think that you're a diva, that you've got too much drama in your life, or that you're not committed to your job.

Most people won't ask whom you voted for, whether or not you go to church, or why you went to the doctor. Just in case, though, you should be prepared with a response that doesn't disclose much about your opinions, beliefs, and experiences.

For example:

- If asked to identify your political-party affiliation, you may want to say that you try to keep up with both sides of the issues and vote for the candidate that you believe is most closely aligned with your views.

- When asked about career goals, you may want to say that you're interested in moving up, but right now (especially if you just joined the company) you want to help the company be successful by being the best team player you can be.

Don't get it twisted: If your supervisor asks you what your future goals and ambitions are, you must discuss them. To avoid the appearance of disloyalty, articulate your ambitions in terms of your current employer to avoid any conclusions that you will leave when a better job comes along.

51   Don't let your ego get in the way. If you don't know, say so.

Regardless of where you are in your career, you're not likely to know how to do everything you'll be asked to do or be able to answer every question you're asked. If you're looking for employment, you should anticipate questions that might be asked as you network and interview, and practice your responses.

If you're employed, anticipate questions that might come up in the discussion or presentation, and be prepared with answers and information. If the questions don't come up and you think the material you have is relevant and helpful, include the information in a question.

You might ask:

- "Have we looked at the impact that weather may have on deliveries?"

- "Do we need to consider whether different time zones make any difference?"

- "Have we considered local customs and practices?"

You can then explain why the information you have is relevant to the discussion.

If you don't have all the answers (and you won't), don't let your ego get in the way. There is no shame in admitting that you don't know. You may be ashamed and embarrassed if you attempt to perpetrate a fraud and get caught. Decide whether to admit that you don't know, or make every effort to find the answer, and then admit that you don't know.

If time is a critical factor, consider immediately confessing your limitation, declaring that you will make every effort to find the answer, and will provide an update within a reasonable, realistic time period. Then you can exhaust all of your contacts and resources to gather the information your boss wants. Whether or not you have it, you must provide an update as promised. Circumstances will dictate whether you'll be given more time to come up with the information and perhaps someone to assist you.

PERSONAL APPEARANCE

Your personal appearance can help you get hired or cause you to be disregarded.

Clothes and manners do not make the man (or woman); but, when he (or she) is made, they greatly improve his (or her) appearance.

Henry Ward Beecher (U.S. Congregational minister, 1813–1887)

52 Your clothes shouldn't enter the room before you do because you're more important than your clothes.

53 Before you leave for work or for an interview, look in the mirror and ask yourself, "Is this the statement I want to make?"

54 Don't be fooled by workplace dress codes that permit "business casual" or "dress-down" days.

55 Emulate the style of dress that is common at the level of the position you aspire to achieve.

When creating or modifying your personal brand, consider that:

- Personal appearance is critically important.

- You only have one opportunity to make a first impression. (It's trite and a cliché, but it's true.)

- Before you utter a word, you can be sized up and judged correctly or incorrectly as to whether or not you are suitable for a position or promotional opportunity.

Is this the statement you want to make?

☑   The Muppets are dearly loved, but Miss Piggy is, in my opinion, an icon. She is known to be a fashionista and a diva, and intolerant of anyone who tries to treat her as other than the star she presumes to be.

For whatever reason, I didn't see or hear much about Miss Piggy for a few years; I didn't give it much thought. Perhaps Miss Piggy was simply off on a personal quest, but I missed her.

Well, she roared back into the high-profile limelight to promote her new movie, *The Muppets,* through personal appearances in 2011 and 2012. She appeared on *The Tonight Show* with Jay Leno and on Chelsea Handler's *Chelsea Lately.*

Miss Piggy, though absent or maintaining a low profile for a time, kept her brand intact and unchanged. Her glorious, high-profile return considerably enhanced and elevated her personal brand. For me, Miss Piggy's crowning achievement was being the subject of a feature article in the November 2011 issue of *InStyle* magazine.

Miss Piggy is indeed The Notorious P.I.G.

Presenting the appropriate appearance as you search for a job or compete for a promotional opportunity is essential. Your attire should send a silent but emphatic message that you're the person to hire or promote.

What is appropriate? This depends on the industry, business culture, geographic location of the business, and the position itself. It also depends on the people who will make the decision about who will be hired or promoted.

- If your preference is to dress like an entertainer, and you're applying for a job as a teacher or a lawyer, or for a position in a conservative Fortune 500 company, leave the stage clothes at home. Entertainers rarely dress in a manner appropriate for traditional workplaces.

- If you're dissatisfied with your appearance and have been planning to address it sometime in the future, the future is now.

Many major department and cosmetic stores offer free makeup makeovers. At the very least, keep in mind that:

- Whatever is worn must fit well and be neat, clean, and pressed.

- Trousers must be worn up on the waist and with a belt, if there are belt loops.

- Socks must be worn, sneakers must not be worn, and shoes must be shined.

- Depending on the industry, open-toe shoes and sandals may be inappropriate.

- Personal hygiene must never detract from your otherwise appropriate appearance.

- Using too much perfume, cologne, or aftershave in the workplace can be problematic for people with allergies or sensitivity to smells or odors.

- Tattoos and body piercings should be covered.

- Vibrant, quirky hair colors, braids, dreadlocks (unless you're competing on *American Idol* or *Hell's Kitchen*), mohawks, and spiky hair should be avoided.

In other words, before you open your mouth, your appearance speaks for you. Consider these examples:

☑ As an assistant dean, James has consistently lobbied the university that employs him to provide more career-readiness support for its students. An important meeting scheduled for the next day was, in James's opinion, the best opportunity to achieve his goal. University administrators and several faculty members were expected to attend.

He needed visual support for his position because it was clear to him that his speeches and discussions weren't persuasive enough to convince the dean to allocate additional funds to the career-counseling department. James didn't know what he was looking for, but he knew that he'd recognize it when he saw it, and he did.

After surfing the Internet for what seemed like hours, James saw the picture that conveyed his message better than any words he had chosen thus far. It was a picture of the university's students at a job fair that had taken place the previous year. The men and women were appropriately dressed and otherwise well groomed, but there was something missing.

James made copies of the picture and distributed them at the meeting the next day. Those in attendance listened to James as he implored them to support his cause and allocate more money for career readiness.

The dean commented that, based on the picture and the report she had received, the job fair was very well attended by corporations and other businesses looking for talent and students looking for jobs.

James agreed, but then asked her and the other attendees to look closely at the picture and ask themselves, "Which of the students in the picture made them reach for their wallets to hire them?"

What surprised everyone in the room was that the camera had captured the lack of energy of the students in the picture. It was obvious from one student's stooped shoulders and bent head that he wasn't emitting a "hire-me" image. Another student was yawning with his mouth wide open. One woman appeared bored with the process.

Quite simply, there was no energy from the students; instead, they appeared disengaged, distracted, and uninterested. Admittedly, it was one frame—a snapshot on a day when there were many more—but, as James emphasized, the students in the picture had missed an opportunity to stand out among other attendees.

He also reminded the dean that, of the approximately one hundred undergraduates and graduates who had attended the job fair, only four received interviews, and not one had received a job offer.

☑ Michelle is a young woman who was hired to supervise an HR team at a New York City company. She arrived for her first day of work dressed professionally and appropriately in a lovely pantsuit and pumps, with what she considered just the right amount of jewelry.

According to Michelle, "I wore my wedding rings, a silver watch, small silver ball earrings, and a silver necklace."

Shortly after Michelle arrived on her first day, Steve, her new boss, asked to speak to her. Appearing somewhat uncomfortable, Steve said, "Michelle, our company is very conservative. I hope I don't offend you, but would you consider not wearing the tiny gold hoop pierced earrings?"

Michelle "got it" and immediately put Steve at ease by telling him not to worry because she would gladly remove them. For years, she had worn the tiny hoops in the upper portion of her ears in addition to the larger earrings she wore in her earlobes. To her credit, Michelle recognized that removing the tiny hoops was in her long-term best interest.

Decide on the message you want your appearance to convey and deliver that message.

A word of caution to men and women: "To thine own self be true."

- Don't dress to convey a message you aren't prepared to live with once you get the job. If you must express your individuality, wear brightly colored or provocative underwear. You'll know it's there, and a prospective employer shouldn't have a clue.

- Thongs that can be seen are a bad idea for work wear. A thong revealed also sends a message that draws attention away from your stellar work performance and toward your physical attributes.

- If you are a trend-setting fashionista, interviews with traditional, conservative companies are not the venue for asserting your cutting-edge fashion sense.

Take care not to give the impression that you're frivolous because of the trendy clothes you wear and the time you spend focusing on your clothing.

You will appear frivolous if:

- You can't walk to the copier because your feet hurt in the five-inch heels.

- You are irritable because your clothes are too tight.

- You are walking around the office too much because you want everyone to see your clothing.

- You don't like the people you work with because they don't wear "fab" outfits like you.

You may be a fantastic worker, but you are headed in the wrong direction if your clothing speaks louder than your talent and there is the perception that you are focusing on your clothing way too much.

Don't be fooled because no one speaks negatively about your fashion statement. It's difficult to criticize someone's dress unless it violates the employer's dress code or is totally offensive.

So what do employers do? At the very least, they don't hire someone whose style of dress is something they consider inappropriate or a distraction. They also might marginalize employees who don't present a suitable image.

☑ Gina, a recent college graduate, interviewed with a brokerage firm for an entry-level administrative position. She wore a dark suit and pumps to the interview; her hairstyle was as conservative as her outfit.

Gina was hired and performed her duties so well that she was given increasingly more responsibility. Unfortunately, Gina felt constrained by her conservative clothing and decided, "I have to be me."

She adopted a funky hairstyle appropriate for a more liberal working environment. Gina also began to dress in vibrant, two-piece outfits with flowing fabric and floral prints. She was surprised when she no longer received more responsibility and was not promoted.

Many years later, Gina told this story to another woman who asked her why she didn't just wear brightly colored underwear.

Gina responded, "I was young at the time and didn't know better."

She doesn't know for sure that her new image prevented her from moving forward, but she believes that was the problem because the brokerage firm was very conservative.

Ladies

■ If you want to be taken seriously, save form-fitting, tight clothing for nonwork-related occasions.

■ Wear the proper undergarments that suppress jiggles and bounces, and make sure the "girls" are adequately covered and supported.

■ The length of your skirt or dress should be long and loose enough that it will be unnecessary to tug at the hem to cover your thighs.

■ If you're comfortable in the clothes you wear, it's one less thing to worry about.

■ If you want to wear a new outfit, try everything on at least two days before you plan to wear it to make sure that you'll look the way you envisioned.

■ If you don't take these precautions regarding your clothing, your appearance will detract from your performance, presentation, and ideas.

Guys

■ Depending on the type of job you're looking for or the culture of the company you're employed by, facial hair may be a problem. More conservative companies frown upon beards and mustaches, especially on their executives and future executives.

- If you're applying for a position that isn't a corporate role:

    ☐ A white shirt and dark necktie with dark or khaki slacks may be worn with a sport jacket, if you have one.

    ☐ A sweater in a neutral color will work if you don't have or can't afford a sport coat.

- If your career plans include rising through the management hierarchy of a conservative Fortune 500 company, mirroring the general appearance of the company's executives and current high-potential employees (to the extent you can identify them) is advisable. For example, you can wear a navy suit, an innocuous necktie, and a crisp white shirt.

- You may want to drive by the place to check out male employees going in and out of the company parking lot. Whatever you decide, a neat, well-groomed appearance is your objective.

You should be aware that managers, as previously mentioned, may have personal biases about many things, including what clothing is appropriate to wear to work. They may not view your choice of clothing as appropriate for those who should rise in the organization. This viewpoint may not be expressed, but it can be one of many considerations that affect you.

If you have limited resources, shop for your employment wardrobe judiciously. Clothing that looks the same can cost hundreds, even thousands, of dollars more or less.

For example, a white shirt or blouse purchased for $25 may look the same as a shirt or blouse that cost $100. The price tag will alert you that there is a difference, probably a huge one. The quality of the fabric, stitching, and tailoring of the more expensive garment should be superior to the similar garment that cost considerably less. However, for employment-related purposes, the less expensive garment is adequate if it's properly cared for, which includes hanging it up after each use, and laundering and ironing it as needed. The objective is to present an image that causes the interviewer or your supervisor to think of you first to fill an open position.

Male or female, dress according to these guidelines:

- Clean, crisp shirts and blouses

- Well-pressed dark suits, slacks, and jackets

- Pantyhose or tights and dark dress socks (long enough to reach almost to the knee)

- A few pieces of understated jewelry for women; a watch and a ring for men

To ensure that you make the appropriate choice of attire, you should ask a knowledgeable person or have a friend call HR, and then ask a young person whose fashion sense you admire how to make your look just a little trendy.

Perhaps it's a belt, handbag, tie, or pocket square that provides that needed pop of color. If it's a very traditional employer, an unseen pop of color that only you know about will be your secret.

Bottom line: You want to look good, be comfortable, and be dressed appropriately.

56 Don't forget to master the social graces.

Remember that the workplace is a microcosm of society and the world. Unfortunately, the negative aspects of some people's personalities and behavior, such as rudeness, crudeness, or a lack of civility, can be characteristic of individuals employed at all levels in the workplace. Common courtesy, which includes civility and politeness, should be mandatory behavior, but it isn't.

Business events: Company-sponsored events attended by employees and guests who aren't employed by the host company offer another opportunity to distinguish yourself, whether you're searching for a job or are already hired.

Even if you think you hold your liquor well, don't make the mistake of drinking to the point that you relax in demeanor or speech. When you attend a networking or work-sponsored event, or represent your company, you must always be on your very best behavior.

Table etiquette: At networking or work-related events, or occasions where coworkers are in attendance, good table manners are mandatory. Don't reach across the table for anything. Rather, ask the nearest person to pass it to you. Place your napkin in your lap, not under your chin.

57 Always treat people the way you want to be treated and require the same from others.

58 Be courteous, pleasant, and helpful to everyone, including administrative assistants and other support staff.

It may not be at the top of your list, but you know that people should treat others the way they want to be treated themselves. This familiar rule governs or should govern interpersonal exchanges regardless of position or station in life. Sadly, it doesn't.

Managing up and down: Whether you're looking for a job or already have one, don't make the mistake of being rude and disrespectful to administrative and support staff.

Intuitively, you may know that you have to bring your "A" game, and "manage up" whenever you interact with executives. "Managing down" should also be a no-brainer but, for many individuals, it isn't even a consideration. If you think that you don't need to be polite and civil to administrative, cafeteria, maintenance, and other support staff, perhaps you should reconsider.

You may not realize it, but support personnel are the eyes and ears of the workplace. Executives may speak freely in front of them because they are trusted or long-term employees, or because the executives are simply unaware of their presence.

Moreover, administrative assistants can be extremely helpful to job applicants and employees at every level, if they choose to be helpful. It's in your best interest for them to like you because, without your knowledge and because of an actual or perceived slight, these same employees may become formidable enemies.

Your objective should be to establish relationships and contacts that are mutually beneficial. You don't want anyone, subtly or overtly, to fail to take that extra small step to provide you with information or otherwise do a favor for you, if they're free to do so. If you're nice to people, most people will be nice to you.

Personality: If you conduct an Internet search of the word "personality," one of the websites that comes up includes the following personality traits list.[17]

After you review the list, decide which type of person you'd prefer to work with on a daily basis. Some people:

- Are very open and adjust to authority; others have a rebellious "streak" and don't accept authority easily

- Accept and are receptive to what is given to them; others are ungrateful for what is given to them or reject it

- Who succeed are ambitious; others are content and lack motivation

- Are cheerful and happy; others are gloomy and depressed

- Are courageous and brave; a few others are cowards and fearful

- Are decisive and determined; others are indecisive and insecure

- Have faith in themselves; others lack faith in either themselves or others

- Have a friendly attitude; others are hostile and unfriendly

- Are generous; others are stingy and selfish

- Work hard; others are lazy

- Are mature; others are immature and childish

- Are optimistic; others are pessimistic

- Are tolerant and open-minded; others are intolerant and close-minded

- Are confident; others are insecure

If you're honest, you'll admit that the first traits listed are preferable to the second ones. While most people don't have all of the personality traits listed above, many probably have some of both.

Completely overhauling your personality is unrealistic, but making adjustments may be absolutely necessary in order to be successful in employment matters. Quite simply, *you must stand out for the right reasons.* Distinguish yourself from the many, many job applicants and promotion seekers by exuding maturity, poise, and professionalism.

Don't misunderstand: If you're in your twenties, you're not expected to project the maturity and presence of a fifty-year-old, experienced businessperson, and vice versa. If you have to make a change, it'll take work, practice, and focus, but you can do it because failure is not an option. There may be setbacks, perhaps more than you expected, but don't accept failure as a permanent outcome.

Communication: Conveying thoughts, information, and opinions in writing and orally are critical skills in workplace environments. Based on feedback you've received throughout your life, by now you should know whether you have strong communication skills.

If you don't write well, you should make the effort to improve. You never know when you may be asked to write a report, a service order, or a memorandum. Why not contact the adult-education program in your community or online and enroll in a business writing course? It's better to have and not need than to need and not have.

A public-speaking course will also help you develop a skill that will benefit you in connection with employment matters as well as in community and political arenas. Good public-speaking skills are important if you want to achieve success in these or other areas. All means of communication you use for employment-related matters must convey that you are a mature, professional adult.

Hopefully, you now realize that your e-mail address and the greeting on your cell phone and landline shouldn't be provocative, playful, or immature, and you understand why. If you haven't acquired a suitable e-mail address and recorded a more mature greeting on any phone on which you expect to receive a business call, please take care of these things:

- Keep your e-mail address and greeting simple.

- Identify yourself by using your first and last name in your e-mail address and greeting.

- Smile when you record your greeting, so it comes through in the recording.

- Speak clearly and stand up when you record the greeting.

Here are some areas of communication and the etiquette associated with each type:

E-mail

- Don't draft and send an e-mail when you've been drinking. No matter how well you think you hold your liquor, it probably isn't a wise move.

- Individuals you contact by e-mail should receive the same (or better) quality of interaction you give individuals on the telephone or face to face.

- Use the "high importance" icon for time-sensitive messages.

- Don't use all lowercase or all uppercase letters.

- Write your message as you would say it if the person were in front of you.

- Use the rules of punctuation and grammar; don't rely on program features, including spell check.

- The subject line should accurately convey the topic addressed in the message.

- Include a space between paragraphs to make the message easier to read.

- Read the entire message out loud before you press the "send" button.

There are more rules at http://email.about.com/od/emailnetiquette/tp/core_netiquette.htm.

59   Practice cell phone and texting etiquette.

Cell Phone and Texting

- Use electronic devices, such as your cell phone and personal data assistant, considerately.

- During interviews, at work, and during work-related events:

  ☐ Turn off your cell phone or set it on vibrate.

  ☐ Use your cell phone only for important calls.

  ☐ Let your cell phone calls go to voice mail during interviews, and set it on vibrate during office hours.

  ☐ Find a private place to make cell phone calls.

☐ Don't use your cell phone in the restroom because of background noises and the lack of privacy.

☐ Don't bring your cell phone to meetings.

☐ Only text on your time (e.g., lunch hours or breaks).

Furthermore, if you're looking for a job, you should always regularly check for messages left on your cell phone and return them immediately. The message may lead to an interview, which may lead to a job.

It's not enough to check the phone numbers of incoming calls on caller ID. You need to know what the person said in the message left for you. Additional information may be needed, an interview may be rescheduled, or there may be some other important reason that you need to retrieve your messages. Remember to return phone calls as soon as possible after you retrieve the message.

Once you begin your job search and after you are hired, always answer your cell phone, even after work hours. It could be a prospective employer who wants to schedule an interview, or your boss with an assignment that can get you the promotion you want.

Telephone

Each time you answer the telephone:

■ Smile. It will keep you positive and upbeat.

■ Identify yourself; if appropriate, identify the business.

■ Sound professional.

■ Be pleasant.

■ Be helpful.

Don't check your voicemail messages on speaker phone because you never know what your friends have said or the language they may have used.

Handshake Guidelines

- Extend your hand, smile, and look directly into the person's eyes during the handshake.

- Your grip should be firm but not tight. Do not use flaccid or fishy handshakes.

- A good, well-timed handshake paired with a genuine smile is a sure way to stand out, whether you're introducing yourself at a company event or an industry conference.

- Absent special circumstances, such as religious or cultural considerations, be ready to shake hands, regardless of your gender or the other person's gender.

  ☐ He or she will remember that you extended your hand first.

  ☐ The gesture suggests two positive traits: confidence and maturity.

Your brand is the story you project and, by your conduct, reinforce. Who you are depends on who you want and commit to be. The common theme is that you are the driving force.

Once you establish your personal brand and are satisfied that it conveys the message and image you desire, you should protect it. Don't permit your brand to be diluted by engaging in behavior that diminishes your reputation. It is also possible for others close to you to adversely impact your brand, or at least cause people to raise an eyebrow to question conduct because of your association with them. It is up to you to preserve the integrity of your brand. Ask any successful businessperson if this is true.

☑ Executive producer Heidi Klum blinked and allowed a season-eight contestant on *Project Runway*, whose design aesthetic was not consistent with the show's established brand, to win the coveted first-place prize over Mondo Guerra, the viewers' favorite. Mondo's bold, vibrant graphic designs were distinctively unique yet consistent with the cutting-edge impact of prior seasons' winners. By comparison, the fashions crafted by the winner of season eight seemed more pedestrian and off-the-rack unexciting.

Heidi had expressed a preference for Mondo, and apparently many viewers agreed with her. On a segment of the ABC-TV talk show *The View*, actor and comedian Jack Black proclaimed that he and his wife watch *Project Runway* together, and that Mondo got robbed! A print-media article concurred with Black, claiming that the season-eight winner stole first place from Mondo. Viewer defections seemed imminent!

Although Heidi acquiesced to the will of the majority of the other judges in season eight, in subsequent seasons it seemed that, during deliberations and in the final determinations, Heidi asserted herself more emphatically. Perhaps it's merely a perception, but it appears that her opinion carries more weight, as it should. *Project Runway* is a key element of Heidi Klum's brand.

Subsequently, Mondo won a *Project Runway All Stars* competition and appeared as a judge on at least one *Project Runway* show. Fans have been appeased, but only because Heidi took measures to rehabilitate her brand by giving Mondo his due and being more vigilant about protecting it.

CHAPTER SIX

What Do You Bring to the Table? What Is Your Destination?

Now that you're out of school or ready to change careers, what do you want to be?

You've got to be careful if you don't know where you're going, 'cause you might not get there.

—Yogi Berra, former American Major League Baseball catcher, outfielder, and manager

If you are clear about what you want, the world responds with clarity.

—Loretta Staples, a graphic, exhibit, and interaction designer

Don't be afraid of the space between your dreams and reality. If you can dream it, you can make it so.

—Belva Davis, television and radio journalist

60   Conduct a self-assessment.

Whether you've just graduated, are ready to change careers, or simply find yourself unexpectedly unemployed, it's helpful to conduct a self-assessment and develop a career plan for several reasons.

Three of the most important reasons are that:

- You'll acquire a heightened awareness of your talents, strengths, and weaknesses.

- The information you acquire will make it easier to draft your marketing pitch, résumés, and cover letters.

- It gives you the opportunity to think about what factors are important to you in an employment context.

There are a number of articles that will help you gather information and gain insight about yourself. For example, "What Is a Self Assessment?" sets forth a simple, straightforward guide through the self-assessment process.[18] Among other things, the article asks readers to identify their values, interests, motivational drives, what they're good at, and what they enjoy.

You can use some of the information obtained from the material you gathered for your personal brand exercise. Your self-assessment should include:

- What you think of or know about yourself

- The feedback you've received from others

- Your personality traits

Next, review the feedback you've requested. After thoughtful consideration, if you agree with the feedback received, keep it in mind if you decide to complete a self-assessment test.

The data you gathered and agree with should be emphasized in your marketing pitch, résumés, and cover letters, and during job interviews. It should also be consistent, so you convey that you're a confident, well-prepared professional who is exactly the person to fill the open position or to be promoted.

You'll find the Occupational Information Network (O*NET)[19] useful as you develop your career plan. O*NET is sponsored by the U.S. Department of Labor/Employment and Training Administration. The website's database also provides career exploration tools for people who are looking to find or change careers.

These tools will assist you in determining the career path that will be most gratifying based on your interests and skillset. The objective at this early point in your career is to be your own career coach.

Later in your career, depending on your ultimate goal or if you feel that you have hit a plateau, or if you simply want to move further up the company hierarchy, you may choose to hire a professional career coach.

When considering a career path to follow, don't overlook vocational careers, which include the building trades (e.g., carpenters, plumbers, and electricians), auto-body and repair work, and personal-appearance workers (e.g., barbers, hairdressers, makeup artists, and manicurists).

These positions usually require on-the-job, hands-on training acquired through apprenticeship programs and community colleges

instead of four-year colleges. Vocational programs neither cost as much as academic programs nor take as long to complete.

Furthermore, vocational positions aren't likely to be computerized, automated, or outsourced. Economic indicators suggest that, by 2014, there will be a shortage of skilled craft professionals because, although the housing and real estate industries are recovering, more workers are retiring from the building trades.

It's not surprising that building-industry groups are engaged in developing future construction leaders. Given that the path to vocational-career employment opportunities is often more attainable than other career paths, it makes sense to consider whether a vocational career might suit you and your interests.

As you review self-assessment and career-path material, consider the following eight questions:

1. "What are my goals?"

2. "Where do I want to be in three and five years?"

3. "What kind of skills and experience do I need to achieve my goals?"

4. "Do I need skills that I don't have?"

5. "Do I need additional education and training?"

6. "Will I need to relocate to achieve my goals?"

7. "Am I willing to take the steps necessary to achieve my goals?"

8. "Who will accompany me on my journey?"

To answer the last question honestly, you will need to have the answers to the other seven questions. Accordingly, before you choose a career and create a career plan, it'll be necessary to conduct research to acquire the information and data that will enable you to make an informed decision and set attainable career goals.

You may want to be successful but, as emphasized previously, achieving success takes hard work, focus, commitment, and talent, and the ability to take advantage of each opportunity. You should be prepared to face negative feedback, delays, and other goal-limiting experiences that may shatter your resolve and self-esteem. Consider whether you're sincerely willing to do the work and make the sacrifices necessary to achieve your goals.

You'll be able to use the answers to these eight questions and the research data to help you complete your self-assessment tool. Realize that some of these items will change over time as you gain work-related and other experiences.

Similarly, some goals and values will be enhanced or will become more important to you later than they are today. Also acknowledge that the converse may be true. Later in life, for better or worse, these items may not resonate as they do now.

The depth to which you address the first question will make your answer to the second question easier to visualize. A word of caution: You may not be comfortable with your answer to the eighth question, "Who will accompany me on my journey?"

Take inventory. A quotation from Colin Powell, sixty-fifth Secretary of State of the United States and a retired four-star general in the United States Army, contains the following sage advice:

> The less you associate with some people, the more your life will improve. Any time you tolerate mediocrity in others, it increases your mediocrity. An important attribute in successful people is their impatience with negative thinking and negative acting people.
>
> Never receive counsel from unproductive people ... Don't follow anyone who's not going anywhere ... With some people you spend an evening, with others you invest it ... If you run with wolves, you will learn how to howl. But, if you associate with eagles, you will learn how to soar to great heights ... Never make someone a priority when you are only an option for them.[20]

The paragraphs above are merely excerpts from a lengthy quotation from Secretary Powell. His quotation (or speech) also addresses the role that family plays in your future plans, and applies the standard that is used for both friends and family members. You can benefit from reading the entire quotation and taking time to think about its message.

Of course, family members will be on the journey with you, although the influence each family member has on you will vary. You may want to determine which family members are best equipped to provide advice and counsel on how to achieve your goals successfully.

Don't make the mistake of equating success with the acquisition of huge wealth, a lot of bling, and a corner office on the top floor of corporate headquarters. People who are honest, hard-working, and respectful of and respected by others are individuals from whom you can learn and who may have helpful advice.

To answer the eighth question adequately, you'll need to evaluate the people you know and with whom you come in contact to ascertain what, if any, role they will or should have in your forward-moving progress. Ideally, you'll want to surround yourself with people who are positive, reliable, and trustworthy—people who exercise sound judgment and have integrity, are ethical, and who support you.

Because of their relationship to you or your affection for them, family members and friends may be the most difficult individuals to evaluate. For example, a cousin you grew up with, who has substance-abuse problems and a propensity for criminal or inappropriate conduct, is not someone you'll probably spend a great deal of time with discussing your plans for the future. Likewise, you'll have to decide how to handle friends who want to party 24/7.

You may also need to think about whether to keep your constantly complaining sister or brother-in-law at arm's length because he or she is so negative and snarky. You love them, but you're on a mission.

Don't get it twisted: You shouldn't leave family and friends behind because they hit a rough patch or don't share your values and plans for the future.

- Loved ones who, over time, have demonstrated their love, support, and encouragement for you are your bridges to the future.

- If by chance you achieve success, you may not enjoy it as much without such people in your life; you will, however, need to manage these relationships.

If you can't say no to friends who want to party until the wee hours on a weeknight when you have to work or look for work the next day, don't talk to them during the week. Save your conversations for the weekend.

A relative, who is dear to you and who has biases that you don't share (or don't freely reveal), may not understand if you befriend coworkers who are "different" from you. Unfortunately, even in the twenty-first century, there are people who are intolerant of differences in, among other things, race, religion, and sexual orientation.

Likewise, consider whether it's wise to invite that relative to join you and a diverse group of coworkers at the local sports bar to watch the Super Bowl. Think of it as if you were assigning seats at each table at a wedding reception. You don't sit Aunt Maude next to Uncle Rupert because they hate each other. You seat Cousin Melanie as far away as possible from her ex-husband Ethan and his new wife, a twenty-one-year-old professional cheerleader, and place them as close to the door as you possibly can.

Ultimately, it's your responsibility to manage your personal and professional relationships to your advantage so you don't derail your plans for the future.

Take into account your values, skills, goals, ethics, interests, and current passions. Avoid the pursuit of a career that someone else chooses for you.

☑️ Luis earned an undergraduate degree from an Ivy League college. His father wanted him to become an attorney, so, being a dutiful son, Luis graduated from a top-tier law school. He practiced law for more than fifteen years before he declared that he had never wanted to be an attorney and left the practice of law. Thereafter, he pursued his passion for journalism and graduated from a highly regarded graduate school of journalism.

You need to understand yourself, your goals, and your aspirations in order to maximize your chance for success. Begin by objectively identifying your strengths and weaknesses. Admittedly, it is difficult to be objective about yourself. Nonetheless, you should try to ask yourself thoughtful, probing questions in an effort to identify the career path best for you.

YOUR STRENGTHS AND WEAKNESSES

We all have them, and interviewers usually ask applicants to identify theirs.

Whether you know it or not:

- You're not perfect, no matter what your loved ones tell you.

- You have weaknesses.

When you know yourself better, including your strengths and weaknesses, you can direct your energy toward highlighting and showcasing your strengths and improving your weaker talents.

If you're self-aware and able to articulate this information succinctly and coherently without presenting yourself in a negative light, you'll increase the probability of obtaining a job.

To maximize the likelihood that you will be considered for jobs that require the same skillset, but with varying emphasis on these skillsets, you will need more than one version of your résumé. The emphasis will be different, but the data should be the same so that, when you are interviewed, you present yourself as a well-prepared, confident professional regardless of the job you seek.

61 — Develop a plan and execute it.

Career plan: It's time to connect the dots. Your career plan should include developmental goals and timetables to:

- Direct your journey to find a job;

- Determine whether you're on track to achieve your goals;

- Determine whether you need to reassess the long-term benefit of remaining with your current plan; and

- Determine whether your plan should be revised.

Your goals and objectives should be:

- Reasonable;

- Realistic;

- Achievable; and

- Directed toward a due date or within a certain time frame.

Every career plan should include steps to establish, expand, and maintain face-to-face and online social networks.

Example 1: You have a bachelor's degree in liberal arts from an accredited college, but you don't have a clue about what you want to be now that you're out of school or ready to change careers.

Your interests are varied:

- You enjoy participating in outdoor sports, watching professional and collegiate sports on television (either at home or at sport bars), listening to music, and kicking back with friends.

- You don't view yourself as a leader or a follower.

- You consider yourself an independent thinker.

- You're not interested in recognition.

- You're more interested in getting things done.

- You're relatively inexperienced and know that you may need to be flexible about work schedules, including the hours and days you make yourself available to work.

You've already completed a personality assessment to help determine what your preferences are and to learn more about yourself. Based on your personality assessment, you're a responsible extrovert who is in touch with your external environment.

You now complete a career assessment to guide you toward a career choice. According to your career assessment and based on your limited work experience, you may find a customer-service or a sales position rewarding.

Sample Career Plan

- Immediately learn the requirements for call-center and sales positions by reviewing job descriptions on O*NET.

- Immediately expand your network of people beyond social networks by joining professional organizations (if you can afford it) and volunteering in your community.

- By (date), identify the businesses that have call centers and sales organizations and their locations.

- By (date), identify the states that have the lowest rates of unemployment.

- By (date), communicate with friends and relatives in these states for networking contacts and opportunities.

- Contact your alumni, job-placement, and unemployment offices for contacts.

Example 2: Status (e.g., a high salary and recognition) is important to you. You don't have a degree. These are values you should include on your list:

- You enjoy bowling, skiing, and music. These are the things that interest you.

- You're outgoing, analytical, and typically a person who is the life of the party.

- Teaching has always appealed to you because it's an opportunity to share your point of view.

- You're a skilled debater who communicates clearly, concisely, and simply.

Your values appear to be in conflict with your skillset—but maybe not. You can become a teacher[21] or a college professor if you're willing to acquire a degree or two. It may mean acquiring a graduate degree if you plan to teach at the college level.

If you really want to teach, and money and status are important to you, establish additional revenue streams to supplement your teaching income and to distinguish yourself as a teacher or in some other way. It will take planning and a lot of work over time, but it can be done.

To establish additional revenue streams as a teacher, you may:

- Coach an intermural sport or activity; and/or

- Tutor students in subjects in which you are proficient and that you enjoy.

You may achieve the status you want by:

- Becoming active in professional organizations; and

- Running for office in the organization.

If you're so inclined, and either have the talent or are willing to develop it, you may also become a motivational or public speaker. Obviously, it takes time and experience to become a successful speaker with a message worth hearing, but it can be done—especially if you're passionate about your subject and committed to your objectives.

Sample Career Plan

- By (date), identify a college or university with evening classes, and plan to enroll as a part-time student to acquire a bachelor's degree.

- If you can't afford to attend school, ask for permission to audit a class for a couple of weeks as a nonmatriculating student. Hopefully, this experience should either confirm that you want to continue with your education or that you should consider another direction.

- Determine which colleges offer bachelor's degrees that will permit you to teach in public schools immediately upon graduation.

- Apply for admission to a college or colleges within commuting distance from your home.

- Consider math or science as a major. (There is always a market for these areas.)

- Research programs, such as Teach America, and determine whether this type of program suits you and your plans for the future.

Example 3: You want to become an attorney. You have a bachelor's degree and considerable student-loan debt. You need to work, but becoming a lawyer is your passion.

Career-plan proposal: As you continue to look for employment, and depending on whether you end up working full time during the day or at night:

- Determine whether there is a law school (a state school will likely cost less for state residents) within commuting distance and whether it has an evening program; and

- Consider relocating to that state and establishing residency while continuing your job search.

After you've found a job, find out whether your employer offers tuition assistance; if not, explore attending law school in the evening as a part-time student and working full time during the day, or working nights and attending law school during the day.

62 Remember: There is nothing like the prospect of success and prosperity.

Whatever your goals and ambitions are, you are on your way to achieving success, as you define it, and hopefully prosperity. You want to make career choices and decisions on the job that will not negatively impact your ability to earn a comfortable living.

Once again, persistence, tenacity, and good common sense are essential in order to achieve positive results. Without them, you are not likely to be successful in today's job market.

63 | Whether you're employed or unemployed, attention to detail is essential.

When your supervisor gives you an assignment, listen carefully and repeat your understanding of what must be done. The due date, time, format, and anything else relevant to getting the job done exactly as your supervisor specifies or directs are essential details for ensuring on-the-job success.

If the date and time are not provided, ask for them. Also ask if there are any special instructions about the presentation of the assignment. It's important to know how to please your supervisor with the work you are assigned. The level of your expectations is also important because unmet expectations make for dissatisfied, unhappy, unproductive employees.

For job searchers, making sure that résumés and cover letters don't have typographical errors and do contain consistent information is critically important. Attention to detail is one of the keys to your career success.

Career Assessment and Planning

http://www.quintcareers.com/career_assessment-dos-donts.html

http://www.quintcareers.com/online_career_assessments.html

http://www.careerpath.com

http://careerplanning.about.com/cs/aboutassessment/a/assess_overview.htm

http://www.achieve-goal-setting-success.com/life-planning-workbook.html

http://www.onetonline.org/

http://www.naceweb.org/s09262012/job-outlook-2013/

http://jobsearch.about.com/od/interviewquestionsanswers/a/strenght-weakness-interview.htm

http://www.job-interview-site.com/examples-of-strengths-and-weaknesses-list-of-strengths-and-weaknesses.html

http://www.cvtips.com/interview/identify-your-strengths-and-weaknesses.html

http://www.ehow.com/list_6755299_list-vocational-careers.html#ixzz2UWLLGRJ1

http://arizonanotebook.com/shortage-of-construction-workers-projected-as-veteran-workers-begin-retiring

http://www.martindale.com/construction-law/article_Stites-Harbison-PLLC_1745918.htm

http://rt.com/usa/plumbers-college-bloomberg-mayor-551/

http://www.constructionexec.com/Issues/April_2013/Features.aspx

http://www.forconstructionpros.com/press_release/10915670/construction-jobs-reach-three-year-high-in-march-2013

http://careers.stateuniversity.com/pages/854/Vocational-Training.html

Job Search 101

CHAPTER SEVEN

You're Looking for a Job ... They Don't Call It Work for Nothing!

Each generation goes further than the generation preceding it because it stands on the shoulders of that generation. You will have opportunities beyond anything we've ever known.

—Ronald Reagan, fortieth President of
the United States of America

Opportunity is missed by most people because it is dressed in overalls and looks like work.

—Thomas Alva Edison, inventor

You may not realize it, but you already have a job. Yes, looking for a job is your job. In previous chapters, to set expectations, you were encouraged to spend as much time each day on your job-search efforts as you would spend working on a full-time job. Work, effort, diligence, networking, and attention to detail are all words that should describe your job-search efforts.

The first thing to do is organize yourself, especially your thoughts. Next:

- Consider the materials you'll need along the way.

- Identify the documents you'll need.

■ Create a list of people you plan to contact.

    ☐ This list should expand into a network that continues to grow over time.

    ☐ You should maintain a record of whom you contact, what you send them, when you sent it, and whether and when follow-up is necessary.

Research: Information is a powerful tool. Research the businesses and organizations to which you plan to submit résumés, and become totally familiar with what you learn. Your objective is to stand out when compared to other applicants.

As you survey the market, you want to gather information to best determine whether an industry or a particular employer will be a good fit for you. A good fit includes employers and positions that require talent that aligns with your skillset, experience, educational background, and interests.

Ideally, it's also employment that you genuinely believe will keep you engaged and interested in the work you will be expected to perform. You will need to assess what aptitudes are necessary, the skills and training required, and whether the business culture of the industry and employer suits your personality and work style.

Research and networking will reduce the likelihood that you will be surprised or land in a position that does not mesh well with your skillset and goals. Although you may feel pressure to find a job imme-diately, a systematic, diligent investigation and assessment of the fit of an industry and a particular prospective employer, including their reputation, are in order. This will best prepare you to be most effec-tive in the interviewing process and help you screen out situations where the culture and job fit will not be in your best interest.

Follow prospective employers online, on social networks, on tele-vision and radio, and in trade publications that pertain to the indus-tries, businesses, and organizations in your areas of interest. Often, these publications contain listings for job openings. They also pro-vide information about companies, such as whether they are laying off employees or planning to increase staff. Be sure to keep your focus on potential employers that you want to work for and that might be interested in your skillset.

Two important directories to review are:

- The *Directory of Associations*, which lists all associations/ organizations and their departments, principal officers, and contact information

- The *Directory of Executive & Professional Recruiters*, which provides a comprehensive listing of recruiters and each firm's specialty, including contact information

These directories are usually available at college career centers and public libraries. If they don't have them, find the organization on the Internet, contact it directly, and tell whomever responds that you are looking for a job and can't afford to pay for the directory.

Ask for assistance, but remember that they aren't obligated to help you. Perhaps whomever you speak to can give you the name of a local contact who may let you use a directory.

Additionally, you should:

- Conduct an Internet search of your area of experience, expertise, or interest. You'll probably identify unfamiliar publications, persons, and firms that can be helpful to you.

- Make a list of material pertinent to your area of interest, including contact possibilities.

- Contact professional organizations in your field and attend their meetings. These organizations often hold meetings that provide networking opportunities. You can never have too many leads.

- Prepare a list of career job sites that are applicable to your field as well as sites that are more general.

- Make it a habit to check these sites every day and apply for positions for which you're qualified. It's important to check them regularly, but don't spend too much time on these sites.[22]

You have a great deal to do, but don't neglect the maintenance of an up-to-date backup of your job-search materials, just in case something is misplaced.

Next, make a list of the items you need:

- References

    ☐ Identify the people you plan to ask to give you professional and personal references.

    ☐ Request the proper spelling of their names and titles. If possible, obtain business and cell phone numbers and e-mail and business addresses.

    ☐ Make sure to contact these people to ask them if they'll give you a reference.

        - Don't presume that they will.

        - If they agree, discuss what they plan to say about you.

        - Make sure to send a thank-you note.

- Résumés (different formats)

- Cover letters

- Network contact list, including the names of people to contact

- A deep background check on yourself to discover what it contains and to verify its accuracy

- Writing sample or sample presentation

All of the items listed above should be in final form before you begin your job search because you'll want to send out material as soon as you get a job lead. A list will keep you organized as well as help you prepare for interviews and send follow-up thank-you letters. You may decide to include additional items on your list, but you get the idea.

Now that you have prepared a list of tasks that you need to perform in order to find your next position, set a goal for yourself. For example, your goal might be that you'll send out X number of résumés and make X number of calls each weekday.

Remember: People can't hire you if they don't know you're available.

64 Seek employment with employers who encourage and value ethics and integrity.

"Ethics" means different things to different people. At its foundation, it is the belief that civilized people should conduct themselves with honesty and integrity. This code of conduct dictates that individuals decide what is right and wrong and how they will live their lives. There are shades of gray where ethical considerations are involved, but the gray areas should not overwhelm the clearly right and wrong.

The objective of your employment search is to have a successful career with an employer who is, among other things, profitable, stable, and ethical. The research you conduct about prospective employers should give you some indication of the profitability and stability of the company as well as if there are published reports or court records about the company that raise ethical or other concerns.

After you're hired, pay attention to whether there is conduct in the workplace that may be unethical. For example, if you hear phrases that describe your employer's workplace as "an audit-rich environment," consider the description a red flag. Try to find out more by monitoring online references to your company.

Don't get it twisted: Don't conclude that your employer is disreputable based only on what may be a stray comment. Rather, pay attention to what goes on around you, and make plans as the situation dictates.

Ask yourself:

- Are the communications between senior executives and employees consistent with their actions, or do they say one thing and do another?

- Do your coworkers say that they're not employees because, among other things, they're not receiving benefits but have been working for the company and by your side for more than two years?

- Are there coworkers who speak with a heavy accent or don't speak English at all working with you for more than a year?

- Do you have firsthand knowledge or is there otherwise reliable information that senior management lies to employees, customers, and stockholders?

- Are there hourly employees who work overtime but don't receive overtime pay?

- According to the office grapevine (which, by definition, is not always reliable), does your employer engage in criminal conduct, such as giving kickbacks to third parties, bribing public officials, or filing false information on financial reports?

If the answer is yes to one or more of these questions, you may be employed by a business that is violating federal and state laws in connection with securities regulations, immigration and/or wage and hour matters.

If you're asked to engage in conduct that violates (or that you reasonably believe violates) a criminal or civil law, you should calmly and politely excuse yourself because you're not feeling well, leave, and find someone to advise you. It should not be anyone from work.

The American Bar Association and your state's bar association should be able to provide you with a list of attorneys who specialize in the area of the law at issue. Also check to determine whether the local law school has a clinic program in which law students with supervision handle legal matters.

If your suspicions are true, begin to plan your exit.

65 | If you have a disability, decide when or whether to disclose it.

If you're a person with a disability, who meets the qualifications of the position for which you applied, you'll need to decide when or whether to disclose your disability to a prospective employer. The dilemma is whether to disclose a disability that isn't discernible during an interview before you're offered a job.

The dilemma exists for several reasons. For example, a disabled person may not need an accommodation (as the law allows) every day because his or her disability (such as a medical condition) may be in remission. Many times, when people feel better, they tend to think their condition is no longer active or an issue; unfortunately, they may be wrong.

Another reason is that, despite the legal prohibition against discrimination, there are some unscrupulous employers who will not hire individuals because they are disabled. These employers, who know better, will offer another reason for not hiring you.

There are numerous employers who not only abide by the law but also actively recruit diverse candidates, including individuals with disabilities. You should be able to identify these employers during your information-gathering activities.

Consider this scenario: You choose not to disclose your disability to a prospective employer who extends an offer of employment, which you accept. You later need a reasonable accommodation to be able to continue doing your job.

> A reasonable accommodation is any modification or adjustment to a job or the work environment that will enable a qualified applicant or employee with a disability to participate in the application process or to perform essential job functions.
>
> Reasonable accommodation also includes adjustments to ensure that a qualified individual with a disability has rights and privileges in employment equal to those of employees without disabilities.[23]

Your new employer may feel that you were less than honest (especially if you would have been hired anyway) because you failed to disclose your disability.

If or when you disclose your disability, you should be prepared to:

- Advise the employer that you need a reasonable accommodation.

- Suggest what the accommodation might be.

- Discuss other possible reasonable accommodations with the employer.

If you decide to disclose your disability during an interview, one approach is to list the advantages of hiring a disabled person, such as:

- They've learned to be flexible.

- They're able to overcome adversity.

- They're problem solvers.

- They've trained themselves to adapt to their environment.

Prepare a list of famous, successful people who have or had disabilities. If possible, identify well-known people with the same or similar disability as you have.[24] It'll have more impact.

Persons with Disabilities

Book

Daniel J. Ryan, *Job Search Handbook for People with Disabilities.* http://www.amazon.com/Job-Search-Handbook-People-Disabilities/dp/1563709899

Websites

http://www.provenrésumés.com/disable.html

http://www.quintcareers.com/disabled_career_resources.html

http://www.rileyguide.com/abled.html

http://career-advice.monster.com/résumés-cover-letters/careers.aspx

http://abilityrésumé.com

http://www.learningrx.com/quotes-from-famous-people-with-learning-disabilities-faq.htm

http://yeswecanbahamas.webs.com/quotesbypersonswithdisabilities.htm

66 Don't appear desperate when interviewing for a job.

When you appear for a job interview, it's a given that you're either interested in a specific position or you're exploring the possibility of a position whether or not you know the details of the job description.

As an applicant, you want to be confident about your strengths and be able to articulate your weaknesses and how you're working on them. Look at the personal branding and self-assessment work you've done to identify your strengths and weaknesses.

You're well aware that the employer holds all the cards or power, but you want to try to level the playing field. Admittedly, your financial situation may necessitate that you find a job as quickly as possible to avoid dire predicaments.

If that is not the case, consider this approach: Tell the interviewer that you're very interested in learning about the position. Also say that you want to make sure that this is the right job for you, and that you're the right person for the job, because you're looking for a role that will permit you to make a substantive contribution. You don't think that is likely to happen if you're a square peg in a round hole.

If you don't think the current economy is the most propitious time to use this approach, put it in your arsenal for use later in your career when you're in a better position to use it.

67 Seriously consider a temporary position.

A few years ago, a *Business Week* article entitled "The Disposable Worker"[25] reported that "Companies that turned labor into a just-in-time, flexible factor of production won't return to an old-fashioned job-for-life arrangement." The article states that more jobs will be "freelance and temporary,"[26] and jobs now offshored to foreign countries will remain there.

If *Business Week* is correct, ask yourself whether you should wait around for a permanent position that may not come for a year or more. Temporary or "nonstandard" workers—otherwise known as independent contractors, contingent workers, and freelancers—don't receive health insurance, retirement benefits, sick and vacation days, severance, or unemployment benefits—but they do get paid.

Federal and state laws attempt to prevent the illegal, abusive use of temporary workers; unfortunately, the abuses continue. If you accept a temporary position, you may find yourself thrust into a situation that requires you to make a decision.

Consider this scenario: You have been employed as a temporary worker without benefits for two and one-half years without any break in service. You find out that, under federal and state laws, you may be legally considered an employee and therefore entitled to benefits during some of that time.

Do you go to your supervisor or the federal or state departments of labor, or do you continue to work under your current circumstances?

Here are some suggestions:

■ Contact the federal and state departments of labor in your state anonymously, tell them your story, and inquire about your status.

■ Call several other U.S. Department of Labor offices in other states to see if the answers about federal law are consistent.

■ Ask for and write down the names of everyone to whom you speak.

■ Do not disclose your name or identify your employer or supervisor.

■ Do not place the call from work, home, or where caller identification can identify the source. You are merely on an information-gathering mission.

Before you decide what to do, make sure that you have adequate information to make an informed decision. If you complain, your employer might terminate your employment. If you were employed in violation of wage and hour laws, you may be entitled to return to your position with back pay, but it could take weeks, months, or even longer.

Your job search begins: In times of high unemployment and under-employment, when there is keen competition for a limited number of positions, it's important to use all available resources as effectively as possible.

One such resource is the Internet because it contains a wealth of useful (and many times free) content that will be invaluable as you search for employment.

The Your Employment Matters website, www.youremployment-matters.com, is a one-stop, job-search, career-planning, and advice resource designed to facilitate the retrieval of employment-related information from the Internet. You can be directly linked to websites, including job boards, articles, blogs, videos, and books that will assist you in your job search or in moving up in your current position.

Spend a day or two surfing the Internet in order to identify additional websites that will be helpful to you.

68 Looking for a job takes work (e.g., time, effort, focus, and follow-up).

Opportunities are usually disguised by hard work, so most people don't recognize them.

—Ann Landers, advice columnist

In a recession, and when unemployment is otherwise high, you'll have to do more than just show up to find a job. Available, let alone desirable, positions aren't as plentiful as you've probably heard they used to be.

Once you make the commitment to put in the time and effort required, how you conduct your job search will depend on your financial situation. Varying economic circumstances will necessarily result in different approaches and a different mindset. If, however, you're a step away from being homeless, anxiety and desperation are difficult to mask.

Not at the end of your rope? If you're in the position to do so:

- Select businesses at which you would like to work.

- Visualize what you want your working environment to look like.

  ☐ Are there offices, cubicles, or open spaces?

  ☐ Is the available position located in the city or the suburbs?

  ☐ How will you get to work? Make sure you have an alternate plan.

  ☐ How are employees dressed? Is there a dress code?

  ☐ Imagine how you want a typical workday to feel.

  ☐ Think about whom you might know who works there.

  ☐ If you don't know anyone, visit the business in advance and try to speak to employees. Ask them what they like about the company and why.

At the end of your rope?

> *When you come to the end of your rope, tie a knot and hang on.*
>
> —Franklin D. Roosevelt, thirty-second President of the United States

You're networking, have been on interviews with no success, and are about to be evicted from your home. You're able to persuasively articulate your experience, skills, and attributes because you've been practicing.

Here are some ideas about what to do next:

- Armed with copies of your résumé, hit the streets, restaurants, shopping and strip malls, and large retail stores that aren't in malls.

- Politely and professionally ask to speak to the manager.

- With a firm handshake, look the manager in the eye and tell him or her that you need work and why, and that you'll do any (legal) job to earn a living. (Don't say it if you don't mean it!)

- If the manager is unavailable, ask politely when he or she will be available. Wait, if you can.

- While you're waiting, talk to the employees and anyone else who is around, and tell them that you're looking for work because your circumstances are dire.

- You must be persistent and relentless. Don't lose heart.

Another approach is to turn your passion or avocation into a paying job by using what you have and doing what you can. You may be able to create a job based on a need that has not been met or a problem for which you have an appealing solution. Creating multiple income streams and turning a revenue-generating venture into a job are examples of how creative people can be in trying times.

☑ An unemployed man, who was passionate about environmental issues as well as active in his community, followed his passion and vocation by leading neighborhood cleanups and various types of environmental remediation.

His passion for his work gained the attention of several local universities and government officials at various levels. The resulting collaboration led to an offer of employment from the local government's environmental business partner. He worked himself into a job based on a need that he found in his community.

69 | Résumés must be complete, concise, accurate, neat, and easy to read.

70 | Your résumé should contain key words and phrases that will help identify you as a potential candidate.

All of your contact information should appear at the top of your résumé and should include your name, home address, home phone number (if you have one), cell phone number, and e-mail address. You want to make it easy for the reader to contact you.

If you've been out of work for an extended period, or want to change careers, your résumé should emphasize experience and attributes that make you an attractive candidate for the type of position you want.

With so many people actively looking for employment, your marketing pitch, résumé, and cover letter will need to be exceptional. If you deviate from the expected résumé format, you may send a red flag that you're trying to hide something.

To the extent you can, your résumé should:

■ Use an easy-to-read font, such as Times New Roman, with 11- or 12-point type.

■ Have an easy-to-read bulleted format, which is usually preferred by recruiters and executives.

■ Be limited to one or two pages.

- Highlight your employment experience and education.

The body of the résumé should:

- Start with your most recent job.

- Include a brief description of your responsibilities and achievements.

- List at the bottom your education and date of graduation as well as any awards you have received and volunteer work.

- List at the bottom your computer skills because it is one of the first things prospective employers want to know.

When completing résumés and employment applications, as previously stated, it's important to pay attention to details.

- Dates are very important, so don't guess about them if you can avoid it.

- If necessary, and for the sake of accuracy, look for documents that will help you reconstruct your prior employment history, addresses, and educational information.

- Never include inaccurate or embellished information on your résumé.

- If you are unsure of a date, name, or address, indicate your uncertainty by using "approximately" or "approx." on your résumé or employment application.

- If you need two pages because you can't reasonably include all of your employers, education, and other relevant information, then use two pages.

- Avoid anything that may indicate that you have not provided complete, accurate information.

Recruiters use computer-generated database searches, which focus on key words and phrases found in job descriptions; for more experienced candidates, key words are used in management theories and concepts. Accordingly, your résumé should contain words and phrases in the job description of the position for which you are applying.

For example, if the description says that the employer is looking for a candidate who can be a "strategic partner" or someone with a "proven track record," "analytic capability," or "leadership skills," these phrases should be used to describe you—either through the jobs you held previously or through nonwork-related activities and your personality.

As you progress with your job search, depending on the position for which you are applying, you may find that you will need to create multiple versions of your résumé in order to emphasize different skills.

Be prepared to tailor your résumé to each job description. Here are a few additional items to keep in mind:

- Be sure that your résumé is accurate and proofread before you submit it.

- If you know a human-resources professional, ask her/him to evaluate your résumé.

- Résumés must be neat and contain no typos. Someone other than you should proofread it before you distribute it.

71 Include a cover letter with your résumé unless you're told not to do so.

Your cover letter should:

- Identify you and the job for which you're applying;

- Describe why you are interested in the position, and how you would be an asset and add value; and

- If applicable, identify the person who referred you.

If the recruiter doesn't want a cover letter, it can be discarded. Consider this rule of thumb: When in doubt, follow tradition. Put another way, it's better to have and not need than to need and not have.

It isn't necessary to provide much detail, but you will want to list some of the skills you have that meet the requirements of the position. You also want to keep it short and interesting, and make sure it's well written. The objective is to make the reader interested enough to read your résumé and invite you in for an in-person interview, or at least a telephone interview.

INTERVIEWING

Consider the questions you may be asked and practice your answers. Ask intelligent questions, which you sincerely want answered and which demonstrate that you've taken the time to prepare for your interview.

Preparation: At the end of this chapter and in the Career Toolkit, Internet resources that provide sample interview questions are identified for your consideration. At least one person has reported that interview questions found on the Internet, in this book, and on www.youremploymentmatters.com were used in her actual interview.

You don't want to miss an opportunity to shine in an interview simply because you didn't take the time to check out the resources identified for you. Practice, practice, practice!

Telephone interviews: If you think that, because telephone interviews are less formal than in-person interviews, you can take a more relaxed approach to preparing for and participating in the interview, you're wrong.

Telephone interviews are commonly used to screen or narrow the field of candidates, and then eliminate those who don't pass the screener's criteria for moving to the next step. Think of it this way:

Your résumé and cover letter are your calling cards. The telephone interview is your qualifying round for the main event: an in-person interview.

Obviously, the most significant difference between a telephone interview and an in-person interview is that the interviewer and interviewee don't see each other. Accordingly, what you wear isn't important, but how you sound, what you say, and how you say it are very important.

- Get out of bed at least two hours before the interview begins, so you don't sound sleepy or have morning voice.

- Drink something hot to clear your throat.

- Eat a light breakfast that won't leave you sluggish.

- Present yourself as awake and engaged.

- During the interview, you may want to stand or walk around if you can remain focused and answer questions clearly.

- If you can't remain focused, sit at a desk or table.

An advantage to a telephone interview is that you can take notes; however, don't try to take detailed notes. Limit note-taking to one or two words as a reminder for follow-up later in the interview.

Don't do anything during a telephone interview that you wouldn't do during an in-person interview. Take this advice seriously. A successful telephone interview will move you to the next step.

☑ Amy was thoroughly prepared for her telephone interview with a staffing coordinator of ABC Products, Inc., a global company with offices in several countries. She used the company's personal-care products, loved its commercials, and was impressed by its mission statement and commitment to environmental issues. The more Amy learned about the company, the more positive she became that she wanted to land a position at ABC Products.

Amy was ready for her telephone interview because she had reviewed her research multiple times and had perfected her marketing pitch. She knew that she had to ace this interview in order to be invited for a face-to-face interview.

Unfortunately, Amy had forgotten to use the bathroom before the telephone interview began. When she could put it off no longer, Amy not only used the toilet, she flushed it.

Guess what? She didn't get to the next step. No face-to-face interview for Amy.

Just because you can't be seen doesn't mean you can't be heard.

How to dress for an interview: Take the time to research the prospective employer's dress code and business culture to determine how best to present yourself.

As previously advised, be true to yourself and your personal style, if you're unwilling to adapt. If you have visible body piercings, tattoos, and/or vibrantly colored hair, and you are unwilling to remove the piercings, wear clothing that covers the tats, and dye your hair a more conventional color, don't look for a job at businesses that don't embrace your personal style. Your research should provide that information. If you've decided that you're willing to adopt the company's culture, don't change your manner of dress drastically after you're hired.

Whatever you wear should be clean and well pressed. The objective is to present yourself as a knowledgeable person with an appropriate appearance.

☑ Helen arrived for an interview dressed in black yoga pants with a matching jacket and high-heels. She chose to accessorize this outfit with a graphic T-shirt and six studded earrings in each ear. Her eye shadow was electric blue.

The interviewer told Helen that she wasn't qualified for the job. She also explained as gently as possible that Helen did not present a professional image, and gave her some tips on dressing appropriately for job interviews.

Hopefully, Helen took the interviewer's advice.

The interview First and foremost, you must know your résumé cold, inside and out. If you can't, with an engaging smile, comfortably and confidently discuss your background with interviewers, why should they hire you? You must be able to convince anyone that, because of your maturity, willingness to work hard, and eagerness to learn, you're the person for the job.

Make sure to set aside adequate time for your interview, and come alone. If others must come with you, leave them at a nearby restaurant or store. You must not be distracted.

Whether you've applied for a job with your current employer or are unemployed and looking for a new position, prepare for interviews by updating and reviewing your original research about the business, division, or supervisor, and the position you seek.

Review annual reports, business summaries, and articles, all of which you can obtain by conducting an Internet search. Even when you feel that you're ready, practice, practice, practice.

If you're an applicant, determine whether this is the company you want to work for by paying attention when you're on premises for the interview. This will verify the accuracy of your research about the business.

- Do you see indications that the employer recycles?

- Is there material about environmental matters on bulletin boards?

- If diversity is important to you, do you see people of various nationalities and ethnicities?

- Is there a balance of men and women?

- Do you notice any disabled employees?

At the end of the interview, thank interviewers for their time and ask the people whom you meet for their business cards.

☑ When Jane arrived for her interview with a small company's office manager, she was anxious and somewhat abrupt with the receptionist. Her behavior was understandable because she had come to the job interview with her child and her sister.

During the interview, Jane asked the office manager how much longer the interview would take. She explained that her sister had driven her to the interview rather than allowing her to use her car because Jane has a history of not returning the car as promised. Jane's interview was also interrupted when the receptionist knocked on the door to inform her that her child was throwing mini-tantrums.

Jane didn't get the job.

☑ Mary arrived at the interview and asked if her husband could join them. The interviewer declined the request and advised Mary that she would prefer to have a one-on-one interview.

Mary told the interviewer that her husband was very impatient, and that she needed to inform him of the time frame for the interview. Her husband was going to leave and come back for her at the conclusion of the interview, but he needed an exact time, as he was very inflexible.

The interviewer told Mary that she didn't know, and she was free to continue the interview or leave with her husband. The husband decided to wait but sighed and tapped his foot the entire time he waited in the reception area.

Mary didn't get the job.

☑ When asked by the interviewer why she wanted the job, a morbidly obese woman replied that she knew this company had a cafeteria, and the company where she currently worked didn't.

She wasn't hired.

What is the moral of these stories? Never bring anyone with you to the interview, set aside the entire day so you don't appear rushed, and have an intelligent, sensible reason for wanting the position.

Depending on the jurisdiction, employers may ask questions that elicit information about:

- Business cultural fit

- Motivation

- Behavior

- Leadership

- Management skills

- Interpersonal skills

- Teams and teamwork

- Whether you are legally able to work in the United States

Employers shouldn't ask personal questions, which are unrelated to the applicant's ability to do the job, such as:

- "What is your race?"

- "What is your national origin?"

- "What is your gender?"

- "What is your religion?"

- "Do you plan to have children?"

- "How old are you?"

- "Do you have a disability?"

- "What is your sexual orientation?"

- "What is your marital status?"

- "How old are your children?"

Always send an appropriate thank you.

- "What arrangements are you able to make for childcare while you work?"

- "When did you graduate from high school?"

- "Are you a U.S. citizen?"

- "What does your spouse do for a living?"

- "Where did you live while you were growing up?"

- "Will you need personal time for particular religious holidays?"

If you're asked a question that you think is inappropriate or even illegal, what should you do? You have to decide.

You can smile, look surprised, and say, "I wasn't expecting that question because my career counselor said it wouldn't be asked."

If you are willing to answer the question, tell the interviewer, "I'll answer the question if you want me to."

If you are not willing to answer the question, politely say so and give a reason why.

72 Always, always send a thank-you letter or e-mail following an interview.

Your thank-you message should include language that informs the interviewer that he or she, and no one else, could have received this thank you because it specifically refers to topics discussed or mentioned during your interview.

Make sure the note thanks them for their time, and lets them know how and why you would be an asset to the business and to the department.

Please don't forget to customize your thank-you message by addressing the recipient by name. If you were told to call the interviewer by his or her first name, and did so during the interview, use "Dear ___"; otherwise, use "Mr." or "Ms."

73 Face background-check problems head on.

Employers, especially those whose businesses involve access to confidential, proprietary, or sensitive information, conduct background checks to identify undesirable candidates. The definition of "undesirable" varies from employer to employer.

If you apply for a sales position and need a valid driver's license, your background-check report will likely include your driving record. It is no surprise that applicants with driving while intoxicated or driving under the influence records and/or a high number of points may be bypassed for sales positions.

- Don't consider any traffic violation minor.

- Talking or texting on your cell phone while driving may result in a "minor" violation that shows up on your background check.

These infractions may prevent you from being hired for a sales position that requires driving and could affect your automobile insurance coverage.

Jobs in securities or other highly regulated industries are subject to stringent standards related to background checks. Thus, people who have been convicted of crimes that involve theft, fraud, and dishonesty are not likely to be hired in these industries.

Background checks: The information provided on your employment application is usually used to conduct your background check. If your new position involves access to confidential or sensitive data, you may be required to provide additional information. You may also be asked to complete another document or supplement the information you have already provided. Take the steps necessary to make sure that the additional information you give is consistent with previously submitted information.

You have legal rights under federal law. For example, if you are denied employment because of an issue on your background check, you are entitled to dispute it.

Please note that questions permitted under federal law may be prohibited under state, county, or municipal jurisdictions. Additionally, in some jurisdictions, applicants cannot even be asked about arrests that did not result in conviction; however, in New York State, you can be asked about pending arrests. http://www.nolo.com/legal-encyclopedia/state-laws-use-arrests-convictions-employment.html

Convictions versus arrests: On April 25, 2012, the Equal Employment Opportunity Commission (EEOC) issued its Enforcement Guidance on the Consideration of Arrest and Conviction Records in Employment Decisions Under Title VII of the Civil Rights Act of 1964, (Enforcement Guidance). http://www.eeoc.gov/laws/guidance/arrest_conviction.cfm

The EEOC seeks to ensure that arrest or conviction records are not used in a discriminatory way, and requires that employers use one of three methods[27] to defend adverse employment actions because of criminal convictions.

The Enforcement Guidance:

- Prohibits employers from treating job applicants or employees with the same criminal records differently because of their race, national origin, or another protected characteristic;

- Prohibits disparate-impact discrimination, which means that if criminal-record exclusions operate to disproportionately exclude people of a particular race or national origin, the employer has to show that the exclusions are "job related and consistent with business necessity" under Title VII to avoid liability; and

- Offers examples and scenarios to illustrate some of the situations contemplated by its provisions.

You should know that:

- Employers may inquire about past convictions because they're deemed reliable; and

- Employers may not inquire about previous arrests, which are considered less reliable.

Although the U.S. legal system presumes that a person is innocent until proven guilty, arrest records may appear on background checks. Don't panic. Just because you have an arrest record doesn't mean there is or was any merit to the charges. Similarly, because an employer can conduct a background check doesn't mean that the company can do anything it wants with what is learned about a prior arrest or conviction.

There are things that employers can do. The Enforcement Guidance notes:

> Although an arrest record standing alone may not be used to deny an employment opportunity, an employer may make an employment decision based on the conduct underlying the arrest if the conduct makes the individual unfit for the position in question. The conduct, not the arrest, is relevant for employment purposes.[28]

Thus, employers may make employment decisions based on conduct that resulted in an arrest if the conduct:

- Renders the applicant unsuitable for the position sought; and/or

- Leads to a loss of, or ineligibility for, an occupational license or other job requirement.

In these circumstances, an arrest that shows up on a background check may trigger an investigation by the employer into whether the conduct underlying the arrest justifies an adverse employment decision.

Due to the constitutional safeguards associated with criminal trials and guilty pleas, a record of a conviction is usually considered sufficient evidence that a person engaged in particular conduct.

The Enforcement Guidance identifies the following factors as the starting point for analyzing how specific criminal conduct may be linked to particular positions:

- The time that has passed since the offense, conduct, and/or completion of the sentence

- The nature and gravity of the offense

- Whether the offense pertains to the job held or sought

When determining whether there is sufficient reason to deny employment, it's also common for employers to consider the applicant's age when the offense occurred and whether there were mitigating circumstances involved.

If you believe that an issue will surface in your background check, prepare a well-written explanation and practice delivering it, just in case you get an opportunity to explain. If possible, hold onto the explanation until after your interview, which hopefully you aced. Submit your explanation to the hiring manager or the HR contact before you leave.

The person who reads your explanation may give you a chance to explain in person or to prove yourself on the job. If you don't, the background-check issue goes unanswered. The worst thing to do is to lie. The next worst thing to do is nothing. The employer will find out the truth eventually, and you may be discharged.

Expunged conviction records: Some convictions are eligible to be expunged or removed from the record. If an expungement procedure is initiated, confirm that your record has been cleared. You will appear dishonest if you fail to disclose a conviction that surfaces on your record.

As previously suggested, consider conducting your own background check through a reliable vendor before relying on a court order that directs the removal of the conviction from your record. Sometimes the act of removing the conviction is way behind the court order that directs the removal.

Drug tests: Generally, drug tests are conducted after an offer of employment is made. Whether entities may conduct or are required to conduct a drug test is governed by whether the employer is private or public sector, or a federal contractor.

The federal Drug-Free Workplace Act of 1988 provides that any employer who receives federal contracts or grants is required to maintain a drug-free working environment. If you're required to take a drug test, don't do what Mitchell did.

☑   ABC Company offered Mitchell a job contingent upon his successful completion of the company's pre-employment requirements, which included passing a drug test. To expedite Mitchell's start-to-work date, Judy, the HR director, offered to personally deliver the pre-employment package to Mitchell on her way home.

After Mitchell thanked Judy for her consideration, he then said, as if thinking out loud, "I hope that weed I smoked six months ago doesn't show up."

Judy didn't know what to say.

After Mitchell passed the drug test and began to work at ABC, Judy spoke to him about his statement. She told him that smoking "weed" and anything else that could be considered illegal conduct should not be discussed or mentioned to coworkers, and certainly not to a company HR professional.

Hopefully, Mitchell realized that he had dodged a bullet.

74   If you are fortunate enough to have more than one offer, notify other employers that you have accepted another offer.

Once you've accepted a written offer, successfully passed all pre-employment requirements, and have a start-to-work date, you should notify any other recruiters from whom you've received offers that you have accepted another offer.

If you don't have a written offer, you may want to wait until you complete your first day of work before notifying other recruiters that you're no longer available.

If you have an offer but believe that you'll receive a better offer, your circumstances will dictate whether you take the "bird in the hand" or let it go in the hope that your belief is accurate.

75 Negotiate your compensation package strategically.

The objective is to get as much money in your base pay or hourly rate as possible. If a sign-on bonus is offered, politely ask that the bonus amount be added to your annual salary. Typically, sign-on bonuses are one-time payments made to new employees to induce them to join the company. If the answer is no, suggest that a percentage of the bonus be added to your salary.

The more money you can get in your base salary, the better. You will not see any portion of the one-time, sign-on bonus after you receive it, unless you get all or some of it included in the annual salary you will be paid.

Hourly workers should try to determine the pay range for the position and suggest that, based on your knowledge, skill, and experience, a higher hourly rate is warranted. Of course, make sure that you have the training, certifications, etc., you say you have.

Where Are the Jobs?

Book

Ford R. Myers, *Get The Job You Want, Even When No One's Hiring: Take Charge of Your Career, Find a Job You Love, and Earn What You Deserve,* explains why your chances to find a job are better than you think and gives you the strategies to land your dream job. http://www.getthejobbook.com/buy-the-book

Websites

http://jobs.aol.com/articles/2013/08/06/unemployed-man-got-60-job-offers/

http://jobs.aol.com/articles/2013/05/21/good-careers-high-school-degree-careercast/

http://jobs.aol.com/articles/2013/03/05/high-demand-professional-certifications-programs/

http://jobs.aol.com/articles/2013/01/23/global-job-forecast-2013/

http://jobs.aol.com/articles/2013/03/03/in-demand-skills-find-job/

http://money.usnews.com/careers/best-jobs/rankings/the-100-best-jobs?s_cid=art_btm

http://www.nytimes.com/2013/03/07/business/economy/despite-job-vacancies-employers-shy-away-from-hiring.html?_r=0

http://jobs.aol.com/articles/top-10-companies-hiring/

http://jobs.aol.com/articles/2013/01/29/best-paying-college-majors/

http://jobs.aol.com/articles/2012/08/30/the-highest-paying-part-time-jobs-in-america/

http://www.salary.com/12-jobs-on-the-brink-will-they-evolve-or-go-extinct/slide/3/

http://jobs.aol.com/articles/2013/01/31/high-paying-jobs-that-dont-require-a-bachelors-degree/

http://jobs.aol.com/articles/2012/12/14/best-jobs-bachelors-degree-pay-benefits-2013/

http://www.thefiscaltimes.com/Articles/2012/01/12/The-10-Best-Cities-for-Young-People-to-Find-Jobs.aspx#page1

http://www.cvtips.com/career_advice_forum/entries/450-What-Jobs-are-in-Demand

http://www.ehow.com/how_5415404_control-job-hunt.html

http://www.cvtips.com/career_advice_forum/entries/389-Stop-Applying-to-100-Jobs!

Career Planning & Advice

CHAPTER EIGHT

On the Job

The key to unlocking my potential is within me. It is in the power of my thought, my vision, and my commitment.

—Author unknown

76 Your success on the job depends on you.

77 Be the best employee you can be.

78 Take or make opportunities to discuss the company with more senior employees.

Unless you have an employment agreement or a legally enforceable employee-handbook provision, or you are employed under a collective bargaining agreement or some other legally protected basis, you are or will be an employee at will.

This means that your employer (absent reasons prohibited by law) can discharge you at any time with or without just cause. Don't give your employer an excuse to do so. Fortunately for you, it's a two-way street.

You have a similar right. You can resign with or without prior notice. Remember: No one is irreplaceable. Furthermore, you should not resign without giving your employer a two-week notice unless there are extenuating circumstances.

Whatever you may think, your employment-related success will depend on you and only you.

- Once hired, aim to be the best employee you can be.

- Don't repeat mistakes; learn from them.

- Leave the attitude and excuses at home.

- Other people and events will affect you, but you will determine the extent to which you are affected.

You'll make decisions that affect how you'll be treated, regarded, compensated, and promoted. If you treat your supervisor or coworkers disrespectfully, you'll not only be unsuccessful, you won't have your job for long.

Your mission is to establish yourself as a stellar performer with whom people enjoy working because of your positive attitude and the value you add to the team and the project.

- Don't frown, grouse, or make sarcastic comments.

- Continue to rely on etiquette books (e.g., *Emily Post's Etiquette, 18th ed.*, *Gentle Manners*, *How to Be a Gentleman*, *How to Be a Lady*, *As a Gentleman Would Say*, and *As a Lady Would Say*) as reference sources.

You may be asked to attend a business luncheon with a client or be invited to your boss's home for a social gathering, and you'll need the information in these books. If you're polite, considerate, and pleasant to work with, and if you produce a superior work product, you should do well.

If you're not successful at work, despite the previous list of attributes, you can decide that you've had enough, look for another job, and, when you find one, resign.

79 You're not better than anyone else, and no one is better than you are.

80 Authority is not always handled well by everyone who has it.

81 Respect authority and the chain of command.

82 When possible, avoid toxic people.

If you've never been told that you're special or been made to feel that you are, then begin by embracing the truth that you're not better than anyone else and no one is better than you are.

Regardless of how you view yourself, it's important that "respect" be your touchstone in the employment environment and elsewhere. It should be a permanent element of your personal brand. Respect for yourself, others, and the company or business for which you work or want to work are prerequisites for success in the workplace.

- Always speak to coworkers in a respectful tone, regardless of level, title, position, or whether you like them.

- Require the same in return.

- Don't let your ego make you think you're better than someone because it gets you nowhere and only makes you look insecure.

It's not a one-way street; it's a mutual understanding and agreement to conduct oneself civilly, professionally, and politely. A smile, a hello, or some other cordial greeting can help the person properly classify you as a confident, competent worker, who understands the meaning of R-E-S-P-E-C-T. Conduct yourself in a manner that reflects your personal regard for yourself and others.

83   Don't let anyone diminish your self-esteem.

As stated earlier, you may receive negative feedback about your performance and your promotion prospects. If you do, consider all feedback offered to be a gift and accept it graciously. You should accept it, but you should not let it make you feel inferior.

According to historian, author, and journalist Carter G. Woodson:

> If you can control a man's [or woman's] thinking, you don't have to worry about his actions ... If you can make a man believe that he is inferior, you don't have to compel him to seek an inferior status, he will do so without being told.[29]

Regardless of your race, gender, age, religion, gender identity, disability, ethnicity, or national origin, you can develop a feeling of inferiority in a work environment if you allow it. Bullies come in all races, genders, religions, and ages—and even adults can be bullies.

Don't let anyone intimate or bully you. Don't let anyone get into your head, so that you feel inferior or intimidated.

84   Continue to research your employer after you're hired.

85   Look for creative ways to position yourself, so that your potential is recognized.

Locate the research you conducted about your new employer in preparation for your job interviews. This material should become part of a file that you create to maintain ongoing information about your employer.

- Continue to search the Internet regularly.

- Check the company's website for information.

- Read company-generated material to shareholders, the media, and professional organizations about business strategies.

- Attend evening meetings of relevant professional organizations.

- Visit professional organization websites to obtain material about topics discussed at meetings.

You don't have to spend money on subscriptions. Go to the library to read relevant business and trade publications to keep abreast of what is going on in your industry. The better informed you are, the better you'll be able to discuss your employer's business and to ask appropriate, intelligent questions.

The information you gather, the discussions you initiate, and the questions you ask will help you engage in self-promotion.

- Volunteer for assignments and initiatives that have a company-wide reach.

- Volunteer for company events that may be related to charities.

You'll meet new people at your company and show that you are a generous person, who is willing to help in any situation. Your objective is to work hard, produce exceptional results, and be so personable that you get yourself on the radar screen of influential company decision makers, managers, and administrative personnel.

86 Learn your employer's abbreviations, language, and business culture.

Employers use abbreviations and other shortcuts to communicate with employees. You need to learn:

- The shortcuts your employer uses

- What they mean

- How to use them appropriately

Your employer may have company-wide initiatives with which you should also be familiar. For example, concepts (e.g., emotional intelligence and critical thinking) and tests and assessment tools (e.g., the Myers-Briggs Type Indicator) may be used by your company to improve worker productivity and effectiveness.

The Internet provides a wealth of information about these tools. It's to your benefit to become familiar with them.

87 If you pay attention, people will show their true colors. When they do, reassess your opinion of and your relationship with them; you may regret it if you don't.

People aren't always as they seem. Not everyone is a good judge of character nor does everyone have sound judgment. If discerning situations and people isn't your strong suit, you have to find a method of identifying people who are untrustworthy, schemers, or scammers. These are people who mean you no good; moreover, no good will come from you letting this kind of individual get close to you.

It's also helpful to identify liars, cheats, "frenemies," and unethical characters. Ask yourself:

- "Would a friend or supporter behave toward me as this person does?"

- "Have I witnessed a person taking credit for work that I know he or she did not do?"

- "Have I heard some of my coworkers say things that are simply untrue?"

Unfortunately, management types—as well as coworkers—may fall into these categories. It's important to try to protect yourself from these dangerous coworkers by creating a paper trail of e-mails, notes, memos, and letters to support your recollection of events.

You should realize, however, that you may not be able to avoid such a person if he or she is your supervisor. One possible approach is to get a mentor to help you strategize about how to handle people who may not be in your corner. A mentor is someone whose judgment and professionalism you respect and whose knowledge of work situations may be helpful to you.

A good manager is a man who isn't worried about his own career but rather the careers of those who work for him.

—H. S. M. Burns (1900–71), British
President of Shell Oil Company

88 Make your supervisor look good.

89 Don't try to teach your supervisor that you have a better style; it usually doesn't work.

90 If you have one approach and your supervisor has another, it's recommended that you change.

You don't have to be on the job long before you understand that the workplace isn't all about you. It is, however, mostly about your supervisor.

In addition to delivering the best job performance, your primary objective is to make your supervisor's job easier and help him or her (and you) look good.

For example:

- Avoid asking your boss a lot of questions; instead, try to get your questions answered elsewhere.

- Anticipate every possible question your boss or others may ask about your presentation or project, and be prepared to answer them.

- Always have a solution to challenges when you present them.

- Don't say things like, "They didn't call/e-mail me back, so I don't know."

- Present the situation, but then offer a solution; otherwise, you appear helpless and unable to think for yourself.

- If you're scheduled to meet with your supervisor:

  □ Call to make sure he or she is on schedule;

- [ ] Ask when your meeting should end, so that your supervisor doesn't fall further behind;

- [ ] Always be prepared for a meeting by reviewing any documents that may be necessary, and have the material fresh in your mind;

- [ ] Understand what your boss expects from you and what you bring to the table; and

- [ ] Push back or disagree with your supervisor and others tactfully.

- Being resourceful makes you valuable.

- Based on meetings and discussions, you may be able to anticipate what your supervisor will need from you before it's requested.

- Be sure to ask before beginning the work to confirm that you're correct and should proceed.

- Deliver outstanding results that exceed your supervisor's expectations.

- Volunteer to represent your group on company initiatives and committees, so that your boss doesn't have to spend time on these tasks. If possible, select the initiative or committee that has the most influential sponsors.

When you and your supervisor meet to discuss your project or any other topic, set forth your opinion or position concisely, in an organized fashion, and articulately. Coworkers may share their opinions on the project or topic but, in the end, go with your gut—even if it wasn't the popular choice. Just be sure that you have a sound basis for your position, and be able to defend it.

You have an especially good chance of being successful if:

- You're a reliable, competent, hard-working person;

- You're pleasant to work with;

- You "think outside the box" or can learn to think that way; and

- A creative approach to problem solving is part of your DNA.

You should:

- Remain informed about the business.

- Be courteous and pleasant.

- Leave your ego and attitude at home, but bring your pride and self-esteem to work.

- Arrive ready to work on the days you're scheduled to work, which may mean arriving early to get breakfast out of the way regardless of what other employees do.

- Be accountable for your performance and your conduct.

- Identify what sets you apart from other employees (e.g., technological skills, writing skills, public speaking, and research) and improve those skills.

- Have a "can-do/will do" attitude.

- Follow through and follow up.

- Don't:
  - ☐ Be a clock-watcher
  - ☐ Be late to meetings
  - ☐ Text during meetings

☐   Miss appointments

Don't get it twisted: If, after hearing your opinion, your supervisor disagrees and you push back tactfully, but he decides to pursue another course of action, then retreat. Learn to tell when the discussion is over and the decision is made.

Telltale signs include the following:

■   Body language (arms folded or the person stands up)

■   Facial expressions

■   Words or phrases like "I'm done," "I've heard enough," and "Enough"

91   Don't overcommit and underdeliver.

It's crucial to meet deadlines; however, if you feel that you can't meet a deadline:

■   Notify your manager in advance.

■   Update him or her on the status of the project and what challenges you may be facing to meet your deadline.

One form of professional suicide occurs if you tell your boss that you'll complete a task, assignment, or project by a certain date and you don't deliver. You may get away with it once, but you might not be given future opportunities to disappoint the person who completes your performance review and determines how much of a salary increase you may receive.

It doesn't matter whether he asks you when you will be able to complete the task, or whether he gives you the date by which it must be completed. It also doesn't matter if you have a good reason for not delivering as requested.

Rest assured: Your boss may not risk looking bad by giving you another chance.

- ■ You must deliver!

- ■ Reliability is essential.

- ■ Excuses are unacceptable.

Unless a very close loved one becomes critically ill and is hospitalized or suddenly passes on, you need to honor your commitment.

The quality of the completed assignment is equally important. If you wait until the last minute to begin the assignment, you'll be sorry. Life continually interferes with work. To avoid any mishaps, begin immediately and be thorough. If appropriate, have someone else (with proofreading skills) check the finished product.

92 Don't presume that you're performing well on the job if you haven't been told that you are, and your performance reviews don't confirm that you are.

Generally, employers aren't legally required to give employees performance reviews. (There might be an exception where there is a company policy or a union-contract provision that creates an obligation.)

Pride and ego should never interfere with your ability to be successful in the workplace nor should you rely on your high opinion of yourself to evaluate how well you're performing. Often, employees believe that they are stellar performers without their supervisor's formal input (or in spite of it).

Ask for feedback: If your supervisor hasn't provided feedback about your performance, don't take it for granted that he or she thinks you're doing a great job. Consider making an appointment to meet with your supervisor to discuss your performance and what you can do to improve. Even if you're an excellent performer, there is always room for improvement.

93 If you have a problem with your supervisor or a coworker, assume good intentions unless and until you confirm that your assumption is incorrect.

A distinguished professor advised his students, "When you hear hoofbeats in the hallway, think horses, not zebras."[30] In other words, the most common explanation is usually the correct one.

If you don't get along with your supervisor or coworkers, take a step back and a deep breath, and ask yourself if you are contributing to the problem. That is correct: *you.*

Ideally, you'll receive constructive feedback about your performance prior to your annual performance review, so there won't be any surprises. If you find that you aren't performing to your supervisor's satisfaction, don't immediately think that someone is out to get you or that you're the victim of illegal discrimination. It may be something more mundane.

The problem may be a breakdown in communications or a personality conflict, or you may not perform your job tasks in a manner that your supervisor finds acceptable. You may disagree, but if your supervisor isn't happy with your performance, you won't be a happy employee.

Take time to consider whether there are simple answers to the problems you're having. Ask yourself:

- "Am I arriving to work on time and on the days I'm scheduled to work?"

- "Are there issues with the quality of my work?"

- "Is my attitude an issue?"

- "Am I a team player?"

Of course, there are many more possibilities but, absent evidence to the contrary, nefarious or illegal motives should be near the end of the list.

There are supervisors, managers, and individuals at every level of management who aren't effective leaders. They may be:

- Nice people, but weak or poor managers;

- Unable to deliver negative feedback properly when it is needed;

- Unable to exercise sound judgment;

- People who aren't so nice; and/or

- People who are incompetent.

Yes. There are management types who are simply incompetent, jackass liars. You'll likely find that people who are incompetent are also unfamiliar with the truth.

There are also management bullies[31] in the workplace and coworkers who get a thrill out of making other employees feel small, making hurtful comments, and engaging in gossip.

As any veteran or serviceperson will tell you, unfortunately you have to respect the position the person holds, even if you don't respect the person.

- You must respect authority.

- You must also accept that your supervisor will remain in place until the right people find out the truth and do something about it.

- You also have to accept that this may never happen.

You may be shocked to learn that people in higher positions are not always the best trained, the most knowledgeable, or, because of their conduct, the most worthy of respect or success.

Again, the workplace is a microcosm of the world in which we live, with the attendant warts and blemishes. Try to avoid individuals who give off negative energy or can't say anything positive about anybody. Likewise, don't be surprised to discover that those employed in higher positions aren't better people either. They may have achieved more, and perhaps they are better educated or better trained, but they may still be unkind, unpleasant, and dishonest people.

Never forget that it's equally important that you be respected. If you don't feel respected and valued where you work or apply for a job, look for employment elsewhere.

☑ Janet wanted to surprise her friend Bianca with a special gift to cheer her up because Bianca was going through an acrimonious divorce and was very depressed.

Janet and Don, a young man she supervised and with whom she was friendly outside of work, agreed that he would be a great a "gift" for Bianca. The weekend that Bianca's divorce became final, Janet and Don flew to New Hampshire to surprise Bianca with her own personal boy toy. By all accounts, Bianca was very pleased with her present.

Janet and Don apparently couldn't keep their weekend escapade to themselves because somehow their employer became aware of the arrangement.

They were both discharged for the conduct described because they lied about it, and also because of other questionable behavior in which they had engaged while they were employed.

COWORKERS

It's to your benefit to establish a reputation for being willing and able to help others, at work and elsewhere, as well as for reaching out to new people to make their transition into the organization easier.

94 Cultivate a respectful relationship with coworkers at all levels in the organization and with clients.

95 Help others reach their goals.

96 Connect with new people in the organization.

People active in their places of worship, charities, and civic and political organizations are likely to help or need help with projects and initiatives that may or may not advance their careers. Either way, it's a "win." The best way to move upward is to look for ways to connect with others to help them reach the level they want to achieve. You never know where that relationship might lead regarding future job opportunities.

You can offer to:

- Assist with preparing presentations.

- Proofread materials, if you're a good proofreader.

- Write materials, if you're a good writer.

- Be a sounding board.

It's important that, whatever you offer to do, do it well and on time. If you were asked, you'd probably want someone to do the same for you. Think of it as a form of networking and good karma.

If one or more coworkers are a thorn in your side, again ask yourself whether you may somehow be contributing to the problem. You can't change their behavior, but you can change your own behavior and how you respond to external events.

Consider the following:

- **Reset:** Reconsider your perception of these people. Instead of labeling them as "problems" or "crazy," let it go. Focus on how they make you feel, and try to view the situation objectively.

- **Reframe:** Ask yourself, "What is the person actually doing? Is there a discernible reason for the behavior? Does something or someone trigger the behavior? Can I tell (without asking) whether anyone else is bothered?" Gather data and specific examples.

- **Reward:** Even if you're unsure of what it is, assume that there is a valid reason for his or her behavior. Kill them with kindness and don't let them see you sweat. Continue to be professional and polite. During an informal conversation, tell them that you're aware of their service to the company and ask them for advice on how they think you can be successful on the job.

  Also tell them how much you value their input. If the employee is your supervisor, keep it moving. Try to stay under the radar until the storm blows over. If the employee is a coworker, you might mention that you've noticed some behavioral changes recently and wonder whether there is any moral support you can provide. Do not offer money. Do not lend or borrow money from your supervisor, coworkers, or anyone else in the workplace.

- **Research:** Once you've approached them in a nonconfrontational manner, you may discover more about what's behind the behavior. Perhaps:

  ☐ The coworker has personal problems;

  ☐ You remind him of someone he doesn't like;

  ☐ Your method of doing things is not what she is used to;

173

☐ He doesn't think he has a grasp on what's happening within the team; or

☐ The coworker doesn't even realize what she's doing.

Until you know more about the motivations and the reasons for the conduct, resolving interpersonal problems in the workplace will be difficult.

■ **Regroup:** Engage the coworker more often instead of avoiding her because she gives you grief. Suggest having lunch together. If it's your supervisor, ask if you can meet periodically or just sit down and talk about how best to work together moving forward, so that you are building a great working relationship. Work with the entire team to shape the team dynamic.[32]

If you stop focusing on "problem people" and instead start focusing on what you can do to change your own way of interacting, you'll soon find that the problems disappear. This approach also works for personal issues outside of the workplace.

|97| Provide constructive criticism in a way that will make people seek your input.

|98| Feedback should be given in a tactful, diplomatic manner.

How to receive feedback or input (also known as "criticism") has been addressed. Giving feedback can be just as tricky as receiving it. Generally, feedback—especially constructive feedback—is expected, even encouraged. The trick is to deliver feedback in a manner that does not offend or anger the recipient.

Always begin with positive feedback, such as things you liked:

■ "I like the way you zeroed in on the issue."

- "Your presentation was crisp and focused on the critical issues."

- "You had a tough topic but explained it so simply. I understood everything, except ..."

- "Everyone was riveted by your presentation. It was so informative."

When you've exhausted the positive aspects, move on to the negative aspects of the presentation. One approach is to ask a question:

- "Do you think that the approach in your presentation addresses all of the options?"

- "I thought of an additional option. Do you think that this will work?"

- "We discussed another option last week, but I didn't see it in the presentation. Do you think it's still a viable option that should be included?"

If you master the talent of delivering constructive feedback and offer helpful suggestions, your opinion will become highly regarded, and your peers will ask for your help. The relationships you cultivate with employees at all levels should result in more requests for your input.

99 Find a knowledgeable mentor and/or hire a career coach.

Don't wait for someone to take you under their wing.
Find a good wing and climb up underneath it.

—Frank C. Bucaro, business motivational speaker

You'll need experience and objectivity to help you navigate business cultures and deal with different personalities. After you've been on the job for at least a year (or sooner, if the need arises), you should identify a knowledgeable, senior employee and ask him or her to be your mentor.

Depending on your career aspirations, and if you are financially able, you may also want to retain a career coach. One person is familiar with the company; the other should be experienced in guiding professionals through their careers.

☑ An executive at a Fortune 500 company hired a career/executive coach for his son when he was only a senior in high school. The executive said that he wanted to make sure his son didn't make any wrong turns as he moved through college, graduate, or professional school and beyond.

100 Don't share your personal business in the workplace.

Whether you're unemployed or employed, keep your own counsel, particularly about the details of your personal life. For example, your coworkers don't need to know that your loved one is in rehab or is about to be deported. Similarly, sharing information about the uncertain parentage of your children—"baby daddy dramas" and "baby mama dramas"—has no place in the workplace.

Regardless of whether they should or shouldn't, people make judgments about others based on, among other things, their personal biases, their upbringing, and their experiences.

To be sure that you as an employee are judged on relevant factors (e.g., the quality of your work, your ability to work effectively as a member of a team, and your attention to detail), remember to keep your personal and family life at home.

If you're responsible for a loved one, have back-up childcare or eldercare arrangements in place. This is your personal business. Your problems aren't your employer's problems. This is especially true now that so many people are unemployed, and you can easily be replaced.

After you've worked for a year or more, you may be eligible for job-protected family leave, if you need it. If you find that you can't handle your personal situation on your own, before you speak to anyone at work, conduct research to determine whether you meet the requirements for job-protected leave. There is a "Federal Labor and Employment Law Topics and Employment-Related Legal Issues" section in the Career Toolkit at the end of this book.

Don't get it twisted: Please don't misunderstand. This advice is neither to avoid making friends at work nor to be embarrassed by the conduct or life situations of your loved ones. This advice is not based on making judgments but on recognizing that judgments may be made about you without your knowledge.

Rather, be mindful not to give anyone ammunition that can potentially derail and adversely affect your career. Many rewarding relationships originate in the workplace, but not all of them stand the test of time. "Friend" coworkers cautiously.

☑ A group of young women, who were about to graduate from an administrative-assistant program, were sent on interviews to obtain employment. The program's instructors were sure that the young woman who had received the highest grades and typed the fastest and most accurately would be the first student hired. She was considered an especially attractive candidate because, in addition to her skills, she had a pleasant personality and demeanor.

Within two weeks, everyone except the top performer had received an offer of employment. The instructors couldn't understand it. One of them asked the young woman to describe her interview, particularly the questions she was asked and her responses to them.

According to the young woman, the interviewer asked her, "What would it mean to you if you were offered the job?"

The young woman answered, "It would mean that I could bring my young son to live with me. Right now, he lives with my grandmother in Massachusetts."

Although they couldn't be sure, the instructors believed that the reason the young woman didn't receive an offer, at least from that employer, was because she may have unwittingly revealed (or the interviewer concluded) that she was an unwed mother.

Remember: People prejudge others based on, among other things, their upbringing, biases, limited educations, personal experiences, or knowledge.

101 Don't expect or look for love at work.

If constant praise and reassurance are essential in order for you to function effectively, rely on your loved ones to be sure you get what you need for continued support and reinforcement about your special qualities. Simply put, get your love at home.

Consider the following:

- First and foremost, you just may not receive what you need at work.

- You shouldn't expect that anything or everything you do correctly or even excellently at work will be recognized or rewarded.

- You may think that what you're doing is wonderful and deserves praise, but you may not have access to the "big picture."

- You likely won't know how your contribution will affect the final result.

- What you think is a great accomplishment may not be as significant to your supervisor.

- You are expected to do your job and do it well. That is what you get paid to do.

The rules of the workplace aren't the same as the rules of the neighborhood. If you feel disrespected or "dissed" by a coworker, manager, or executive, and you resort to resolution methods depicted in films, on television, or in your neighborhood, you'll likely lose your job or your employment opportunity.

Disciplinary action may be forthcoming because many employers have zero tolerance for fighting on the job, on the company's premises, or at a company-sponsored event. Insubordination, including refusing to follow your supervisor's instructions or speaking to your supervisor rudely, crudely, or unprofessionally, can also land you in trouble.

It's best to:

- Face workplace situations with a thick skin.

- Make sure that what you perceive as disrespect or a slight is just that, and not an unintentional or ignorant lack of sensitivity or civility.

- Look for teachable opportunities.

- Keep in mind that self-respect and self-confidence frequently can be interpreted as arrogance and snobbishness. Sometimes it's difficult to discern the difference. A smile helps.

102 Keep your loved ones out of the workplace.

"The 'Millennials' Are Coming" is a provocative look at Generation Y (also known as "millennials," or young people born between 1980 and 1995). According to this *60 Minutes* segment, many millennials are reared and educated in a supervised, monitored, coached environment and aren't prepared for the "cold realities of work."[33] If this is true, well-meaning helicopter parents[34] have a nickel in that dime.

The segment recounts how a particularly interested parent contacted her child's supervisor to challenge the performance report her child had received. Take the time to view the segment on the *60 Min-*

utes site, or find it on the Internet. You may find it entertaining as well as instructive about the perceptions related to millennials.

Admittedly, millennials aren't the only segment of the population that allows their loved ones to insinuate themselves into the workplace. The well-meaning spouses and significant others of each generation have also been known to intrude inappropriately into the workplace; the parents of millennials, however, are very persistent.

You should almost never have someone else call your employer on your behalf. The only exception may be if you're too sick to inform your supervisor that you'll be absent.

☑ Greta wanted to take vacation time during the week her husband's plant was closed; unfortunately, another employee had requested the same time off and received approval before Greta made her request.

The size of the staff and the workload required that Greta remain on the job. Rather than accept that she couldn't take the time off, Greta let her husband call her supervisor to persuade him to grant her vacation request. The supervisor appropriately refused to speak to Greta's husband about the matter.

Issues of privacy preclude your employer from discussing (or disclosing) most matters with anyone but you. Furthermore, your supervisor's opinion of you may be diminished by such behavior.

|103| Don't sh*t where you eat.

Engaging in romantic/sexual relationships at work is very risky because consensual relationships have been known to turn bad. Find love/lust elsewhere, unless you are willing to risk losing your good name, reputation, and possibly your job.

No matter what anyone tells you, there are no circumstances under which you are obliged to engage in sexual activities to keep your job. Again, there is a "Legal Rights and Pre-Employment Matters" section on the www.youremploymentmatters.com website, and

"Federal Labor and Employment Law Topics and Employment-Related Legal Issues" section in the Career Toolkit.

If you assume the risk and find true love, one of you should consider finding another job and leaving the company to avoid possible conflicts of interest and to reduce the risk of losing two incomes if both of you are laid off.

☑ An anonymous e-mail, which was sent to the corporate offices of a Fortune 500 company, alleged that a senior executive and a female within his organization were having an affair. The e-mail also alleged that the female had received preferential treatment because of the relationship.

The company's policy prohibits management personnel from having intimate relationships with employees within their chain of command. To determine whether there was a policy violation, the company conducted a formal investigation.

Both the executive and the female employee denied the allegations. Other individuals, who were either identified in the e-mail or were determined to possibly have knowledge pertinent to the investigation, were also questioned. Unable to corroborate the allegations in the e-mail, the investigation was concluded without any action being taken.

Another e-mail was sent to the company's corporate offices. This time, copies of e-mails between the executive and female employee were attached to the e-mail. The attachments contained intimate exchanges, which, if proven to be exchanged between the two employees, would confirm that they had enjoyed more than a professional relationship.

The investigation was reopened. Again, the executive and the female employee were questioned without prior notice. When confronted with the e-mails, one of the employees admitted to the relationship; the other employee still denied any inappropriate conduct.

Both employees, who had more than thirty years of company service between them, were discharged. The company also had a policy (of which the employees were aware), which provided that lying in connection with an investigation was grounds for discharge.

104 Don't engage in criminal, unethical, or otherwise unprofessional behavior on or off the job.

You would be surprised by the number of people who smoke marijuana during working hours and on company property. Consumption of alcohol at lunch (while not illegal) occurs and is also not advised.

■ Work-related social activities should always be considered work, especially if management is in attendance. It seems obvious that social drinking at work-related events should be kept to a minimum. You'll get invited to events where alcohol is served. Even if your boss or others get drunk, don't join that group! Too many embarrassing things happen at holiday parties and happy hours. You don't want to be the one everyone is talking about the next morning.

■ Pace yourself.

■ Have a drink, but then grab a glass of water to remain hydrated.

■ Consume your drink slowly.

You want to be in control of yourself at all times and present a favorable impression about your judgment and professionalism. Anything less may be held against you. It's simply risky to have too much of a good time with friends who work with you.

105 At work, the only place you should expect privacy is behind the locked door of a bathroom stall.

Whether you work in an open-spaced environment, one with cubicles, a combination of the two, or another configuration entirely, there is very little privacy in the workplace.

It's always wise to conduct yourself professionally, especially when interacting with a client. Keep in mind that those around you can hear you. If you want to gossip or talk about personal things, don't do it at your desk. Wait until you leave. The walls of enclosed offices and conference rooms can be quite thin.

Even if you think that no one can hear you, it's never certain; moreover, it looks very unprofessional and immature to see a person whispering. This isn't high school.

Once you get a job, don't engage in behavior that will cause you to lose it.

- Keep in mind that your employer owns the telephones, computers, and just about everything else you use at work.

- Don't expect privacy on any electronic device provided by your employer.

- It's common for employers to have policies that prohibit or limit employees' personal use of company hardware and software.

- Don't visit controversial websites that are not work related.

- Don't use your computer for personal business, including doing schoolwork, conducting personal research, paying bills, or logging onto your personal e-mail account from work.

- Pornography sites should never be accessed at work.

- It isn't unusual for employers to monitor their employees' system use.

- It's better to be safe than sorry.

106   Continue to conduct periodic self-assessments.

After you've been on the job for a while, take time to look in the mirror and determine whether you like what you see. Are you an honest, hard-working person of integrity of whom your loved ones can be proud? If you aren't, you should regroup and make the necessary changes to put you on the right path.

You also want to stay on track with your career plan and your personal brand, which includes checking your e-mail regularly and answering your phone after you're hired. If you don't check your e-mail, you may not have the most current information from your supervisor.

You may not have information because your job or your level in the company doesn't warrant it. Remember: No one has all the information about everything or any one thing.

You may not know why the information isn't available to you, or it may be available but only some of it. In the workplace, as in the military, much information is disclosed only on a need-to-know basis. Your employer may be trying to sell the company, and you don't know it.

The office grapevine may seem like a reliable source of information, but don't be fooled. It would be a serious error in judgment to rely on the office grapevine and then repeat what you hear; it would also be foolhardy to ignore it completely.

Gossip, by definition, is unreliable; nonetheless, there may be a kernel of truth to the stories circulating throughout the office. Don't gossip or rely on it, but don't dismiss it. You may not know what is true and what is conjecture or pure fabrication, but file gossip away in your memory.

107 Loyalty and trust are important but not always reciprocated.

- Companies are not loyal, but individuals should be.

- Be loyal to your employer and your supervisor.

- If you can't be loyal to your current employer, you should look for another job.

- Don't make mistakes that will require your supervisor to defend you to more senior employees. Your supervisor may not do so.

- If you decide to be loyal to other individuals, make sure they deserve it and are loyal to you.

- Don't "throw anyone under the bus" unless there are legal implications or you are asked a direct question that requires a direct, honest answer.

- Take responsibility for your actions and be honest if you mess up. Even if reprimanded, you will learn from the experience.

- It helps to have a friend at work, preferably in another department, to expand your network and expose yourself to different points of view.

As previously advised, you should seek employment with companies that:

- Encourage and value ethics and integrity

- Appear to emphasize practices and ideas that are important to you, such as:

  ☐ Employee satisfaction

☐ Work-family balance

☐ The environment

☐ Community service

Begin by checking the company's website to obtain a sense of its core values and whether there is an ethics program. Media sites used by recruiters, such as LinkedIn.com, may provide great data on companies.

If you have a family, look for statements and information about work-family balance, such as whether there are employer-subsidized, on-site childcare and exercise facilities. Consider the additional issues that are important to you.

If, after you're hired, you don't believe that your employer operates in accordance with the values that attracted you in the first place, don't quit your job until you find employment elsewhere. Your professional and personal reputation is your stock in trade. You don't want to be tainted professionally because you work for a company exposed on the front pages of national news outlets as one that engages in criminal or otherwise unethical activities.

NETWORK, NETWORK, NETWORK ...

Networking is a critical element of your GPS to Employment Success®.

108
After you become employed, maintain the contacts you made and the network you developed during your job search because you never know when you may need them again.

The journey that ends with acquiring a new position typically includes meeting and otherwise interacting with people whom you knew previously and those whom you met along the way.

It's wise to maintain and update your network database. Even if you never need them again for a job search, you may need to reach out to the contacts in your network for support for community, environmental, and charitable efforts.

Remember: It's better to have and not need than to need and not have.

109
If you can't take it any more, find another job before you resign.[35]

Keep in mind that everyone goes through "ruts" and becomes unhappy with their job. This may be temporary, but it's important never to let it show when at work. Don't develop an attitude because you're unhappy.

Your problem is yours and shouldn't be taken out on your coworkers and supervisor. If you are interviewing elsewhere, keep it to yourself.

- Don't share with people at work because it will get around.

- If you're miserable, don't try to make everyone else miserable, too.

☑ According to Bella, who is under thirty-five and has managed several teams that include young professionals, they're shy and reluctant to reach out to executives to ask questions or to obtain needed information. The reason young professionals give for their hesitancy is that they don't know the executive, or they don't want to bother him or her.

Bella says, "I tell them, 'That is your fault. You need to get up and be assertive and introduce yourself. These are not mean or intimidating people. You are letting their title scare you, and they are very friendly and easy to talk to. To me, it is not an excuse to say that you don't know them when it is our job to know them.'

"'You can't expect to be walked around, handheld, and introduced to every single person when you're new to a company. At some point, you have to take control and get to know who you need to know in order to do your job well.'"

Before you decide to resign, consider the following:

- Don't make decisions about your career when you're emotional. Give yourself time to calm down, and think about the situation when you're in a neutral mindset. Sometimes people become frustrated with their bosses, certain projects, or coworkers, and get worked up and decide to quit. This is never a wise decision.

- It's important to be able to handle change and transition in the workplace. Turnover is common and transitions happen often. It's important to be able to "go with the flow" and not get caught up in it. People like to remain in their comfort zones at work and, when leadership at an executive level changes, there may be significant changes that will affect your job. Don't panic! You must be patient during these times and remind yourself that it's temporary. In a few months, you'll look back and realize that you were able to adjust (hopefully).

- Can you afford to quit your job until you find another one? How long did it take you to find the job you have? Have you saved enough money to support yourself for at least a year?

- Don't resign unless you mean it.

If you decide to quit your job:

- Never burn bridges. It's a cliché but so true.

- Depart professionally.

- Don't decide to tell anyone what you think of them.

- Give your employer at least a two-week notice.

- Be flexible.

- Offer to stay to transition someone, if needed. It shows that:

  - ☐ You care about your team's success; and

  - ☐ You don't want to ditch them and leave them to figure out projects that you owned.

☑ Barbara, who has been employed in different areas of the advertising industry since college, and each time left one company for a better opportunity, offers the following advice:

"I cannot tell you how many times I run into someone I knew in another job ... people always resurface, and it is good when they recall you in a positive way.

"Someone you dislike on your team could become your client one day for all you know ... people jump around a lot in careers and you never know where you or they will end up."

Don't get it twisted: Once again, don't quit your current job until you have another one.

189

No matter how well you perform or how much you deserve to be promoted, you can't force an employer to promote you. Furthermore, despite what you may think, remaining on a job year after year does not entitle an employee to a promotion. You have other options.

Look for another job, and do your "due diligence," or homework, about the companies you plan to contact for employment opportunities. In recessionary times, keep the job you have, but plan your departure while remaining on the job.

Make yourself more marketable so that, when the job market improves, you're positioned to move into a job (perhaps with another employer) where there is more opportunity to advance.

- Take advantage of tuition-assistance programs to obtain a higher degree or additional training.

- Take additional training courses to acquire more skills and obtain certifications.

- Get involved in charitable, civic, community, and professional organizations to increase your networking contacts.

- Don't be afraid to "move on to move up" because you can't rely on the job-security concept of yesterday.

"We spend most of our days at work; it is therefore very important that we get along with our employers, employees, colleagues, and clients."[36]

Human resources: Traditionally, HR is the department responsible for recruiting, hiring, onboarding new hires, assessing talent, training, administering payroll and employee benefits, and disciplining and discharging employees.

Depending on the employer's size, organizational structure, and culture, HR may also be responsible for organizational leadership, employment- and labor-law compliance, and mobility management, particularly as it applies to expatriates (i.e., U.S. citizens and foreign-born individuals, who work outside their countries either permanently or temporarily).

Your employer may have an HR policy and procedure manual or an employee handbook, which contains the company's rules, standards, and guidance about recruitment, compensation, benefits, training, and retention and termination of employment. Generally, there is no legal obligation to provide a policy manual or handbook, so some employers do and some don't.

If, after you're hired, you're given an HR manual or employee handbook, and are then requested to sign a document that acknowledges that you received the manual, read the document carefully so you know what you're signing.

Likewise, read the manual or handbook because it may contain the procedural standards and workplace rules to which you will be held as an employee. In some states, an employee handbook is considered an employment contract. Thus, you may have rights that you didn't know about, but your employer also has rights.

A FEW THINGS YOU SHOULD KNOW

Whether or not you've had a job before, you may not know that employees and employers have rights and that employee benefits can be advantageous and save you money.

Employers rights are:

- Identified in employment contracts, including (where applicable) policy manuals and employee handbooks, and collective bargaining agreements (union contracts);

- Implied by law; and

- Imposed by federal and state law.

Employers have a right to:

- Rely on employees' representations about skills and experience;

- Require certain performance levels from employees;

- Direct the work to be performed;

- Expect that employees not reveal trade secrets or confidential information; and

- Expect that employees will work exclusively for the employer during the workday.

The obligations between employers and employees are generally regulated by legislation and case law.

Employees must:

- Be paid for work done;

- Receive equitable compensation (i.e., same classification, same skills = similar wages);

- Be compensated in accordance with the appropriate collective bargaining agreement, if applicable; and

- Receive the same fringe benefits as others in their job classification.

Employers must provide:

- A reasonably safe workplace; and

- Accurate personnel records.

HR can be helpful as you learn your way around the company and learn how things are done. Remember, however, that:

- HR works for your employer and, as such, owes a duty to your mutual employer to act in the employer's best interest.

- Ideally, your interest and your employer's interest will be aligned, but that may not always be true.

- As with any staff, all HR employees aren't created equal; some have more experience and knowledge than others.

Employee relations is a discipline within the HR function of a nonunion business or a business that has both union and nonunion employees, which typically handles:

- Compensation and benefits

- Workplace safety

- Recruitment and selection

- Performance management

- Discipline and discharge

Employee relations specialists identify and resolve workplace issues concerning allegations of discriminatory employment practices, including sexual and otherwise unlawful harassment.

They may also conduct or assist with workplace investigations and address:

- Employer responses to nonunion employee complaints

- Employee engagement and satisfaction

- Turnover and retention issues

- The management of performance-management issues

- The management of employee-recognition initiatives

- Representation of the employer at unemployment hearings

Labor relations is a broad HR field, which includes the multitude of interactions between employers, employees, and unions or other organizations that represent those employees.

- **Open shop**—This is a business in which union and nonunion workers are employed and in which union membership is not a condition of securing or maintaining employment.

- **Closed shop**—This is a workplace in which the employer has agreed to employ only members of a particular labor union. Employees must remain members of the union to remain employed.

- **Agency shop**—This requires that every company employee, who works in a position that is in the union's bargaining unit, must pay the union an amount equal to the union's customary initiation fees and monthly dues or a percentage thereof. An agency shop does not require that an employee:

  - ☐ Become a formal union member.

  - ☐ Become a union member before being hired.

  - ☐ Take an oath or obligation, or observe any internal union rules and regulations except the payment of dues or agency fee.

Labor Relations Specialists are typically responsible for matters involving labor-management issues, such as:

- Collective bargaining negotiations

- Grievances

- Arbitration

- Work stoppages/slowdowns

- Strikes

110   Take advantage of your employer's benefits.

111   If your employer has an employee assistance program, check it out. You may not need it now, but you may need it later.

Employee benefits: The array of fringe benefits available to employees varies from employer to employer. As soon as possible before or soon after you begin to work, review the benefits offered and take advantage of them. Many employers offer the following benefits and more.

Tuition assistance or tuition reimbursement: This is a benefit designed to assist employees who wish to attend college or university classes, so that they may expand their knowledge and skills.

Read tuition-assistance materials carefully because your employer may:

- Set a dollar limit available to each employee annually;

- Establish the number of classes they'll pay for each year for each employee through tuition assistance;

- Require employees to pay for their own tuition and books when they register for classes;

- Reimburse the employee when he or she submits the receipts and evidence of earning a "C" or above grade upon completion of the class; and/or

- Require that the employee sign an agreement to pay back the tuition assistance if he or she leaves the organization within a certain period of time and substantial amounts are spent on tuition assistance.[37]

If tuition assistance is offered, and you don't have an undergraduate or a graduate degree, consider enrolling in courses or plan to do so the following year. Tuition-assistance programs are a cost-effective means of enhancing your skillset and marketability at your employer's expense.

Unless your employer has a policy that provides otherwise, accepting tuition assistance shouldn't preclude you, subject to approval from your supervisor, from also enrolling in training programs offered by your employer on-site, online, or at another location. The objective is to obtain as much training at your employer's expense as possible.

Employee assistance programs (EAPs) are an employee benefit provided by employers to assist employees and members of their households with personal issues that might negatively affect job performance. Short-term counseling and support may be all that an employee needs. Generally, for longer-term counseling and support, a referral to another agency or provider is offered.

EAPs:

- Are frequently, although not always, offered in conjunction with the employer's health insurance plan; and

- May provide needs assessment, counseling, and referrals for employees and their family members when faced with mental health or emotional issues.

Typically, EAPs are available to assist the employee when he or she needs help dealing with life events, workplace issues, and other personal problems and challenges. For example, if an employee's spouse or child has a substance-abuse problem, the employee may contact the EAP to get help from professionals to deal with the issue in a private manner.[38]

According to the U.S. Department of Labor, EAPs most frequently assist employees in dealing with issues in the following areas:

- Alcoholism

- Drug abuse

- Marital difficulties

- Financial problems

- Emotional problems

- Legal problems

These programs typically offer a wide range of support for employees to help them obtain information about some of the following topics:

- Childcare or eldercare

- Short-term counseling for emotional and psychological issues

- Referral services related to situations, such as:

  ☐ Job loss

  ☐ Possible job loss

  ☐ Long-term unemployment; and

  ☐ Evictions and foreclosures that result in anxiety, depression, and hopelessness.

If your employer offers an EAP, review the material to determine whether you can benefit from the services offered. Reach out for help if you feel that you're at the end of your rope.

Don't be embarrassed! Tell your HR person that you're in crisis and you need help. Before you share sensitive information with your employer's EAP, confirm that the information will remain confidential.

Employee stock option plans are benefit plans that employers offer their employees to enable them to acquire ownership in the company through the purchase of stock. Consult a qualified financial expert to plan your financial future.

Employee stock purchase plans are another benefit offered by employers to give their employees the opportunity to buy stock in the company. The plan may be part of a qualified retirement plan, such as a 401(k), or it may simply be a benefit offered by the employer. There are websites[39] that provide basic information, but it is wise to consult a qualified financial expert to plan your financial future.

Consider the following advice:

- It is never a good idea to have any one investment (stock or mutual fund) make up more than 10 to 15 percent of your portfolio, even your own company's stock. Certainly, take advantage of any employee stock purchase benefit; just don't let it get out of balance.

- Anyone who tries to convince or coerce you into buying more of your company stock is not acting in your best interest and, depending on how they approach you, may be violating securities laws.[40]

A 401(k) plan is a deferred-compensation plan, which is established by an employer who pays for the administration of the plan. Qualified employees are allowed to authorize pretax payroll deductions and defer the taxes on the principal and earnings until retirement. Employers may elect to match employee contributions up to a specified amount.[41]

Employee benefits often offer opportunities that can enhance your marketable skills and financial future. It's a mistake to overlook them.

On the Job

http://management.fortune.cnn.com/2013/04/23/bullying-cruelty-work-office/

http://www.ehow.com/how_8516434_make-career-happen.html

http://medixstaffingsolutions.blogspot.com/2011/12/how-to-break-up-with-your-job-properly.html

http://www.life123.com/career-money/career-development/negotiating-salary/negotiating-salary-2.shtml

http://money.usnews.com/money/blogs/outside-voices-careers/2011/05/10/16-signs-its-time-to-quit-your-job

http://gethiredfast.com/2012/06/how-to-find-a-job-when-you-already-have-one/

Career Assessments

http://www.quintcareers.com/career_assessment-dos-donts.html

Promotions

http://www.cvtips.com/career_advice_forum/entries/473-What-Does-it-Take-to-Get-Promoted

MORE RESOURCES IN THE CAREER TOOLKIT!

Save for a rainy day.

SECTION V

More to Consider

CHAPTER NINE

Think Horses, Not Zebras

A Few Legal Considerations[42]

> *Knowing the law as it applies to activities you*
> *engage in is important for every citizen.*

> —Nicolas Eyle, founder and executive
> director of ReconsiDer[43]

Believe it or not, the workplace is teeming with potential legal issues, some that might never occur to you. Consider this story:

☑ Sarah worked at a large, national, tax-preparation company and had been employed for six years. She was considered a good worker, who did her job well and minded her own business.

As usual, April was a hectic month for the company and its employees because April 15, tax filing day, was fast approaching. Employees worked long hours to service clients, and nerves were a little frazzled.

Late one April afternoon, Sarah received a phone call from a client who wanted to speak to Tiffany, an employee who worked down the hall from Sarah. Instead of trying to call Tiffany on the telephone, and because she needed to use the ladies' room that was across the hall from Tiffany's work station, Sarah got up and headed toward Tiffany and the ladies' room.

When Gerard, Sarah's supervisor, saw her leaving her work area, he directed her to return to her desk because the telephones were ringing loudly and incessantly.

Before Sarah could explain, Gerard, who was highly regarded, well liked, and usually calm, took her by the arm and firmly guided her back to her desk.

The following day, Sarah filed a complaint in the local municipal court, alleging that Gerard had assaulted and battered her in violation of the state's civil laws.

To Gerard's surprise, the judge ruled in Sarah's favor. The judge's ruling was probably based in part on Gerard's admission that he had touched Sarah without her permission and guided her back to her desk, as she had alleged in her complaint.

A court of competent jurisdiction made a determination that Gerard had violated a law.

In addition to the more readily recognizable federal and state criminal and civil laws, there are other business and workplace laws and ethical considerations of which you should be aware. Even if you don't want or plan to have a "corporate" job, the business for which you work may be subject to some or all of the laws set forth below.

Corporate accountability: As previously recommended, research conducted in preparation for your job search should continue after you're employed. While it's important to be grateful, don't become complacent because you've got a job and you're content to be employed. Employees of Enron, Tyco, and WorldCom, Inc., likely wished they had been more vigilant.[44]

The Sarbanes–Oxley Act of 2002 ("SOX") was enacted in response to the scandalous corporate conduct by the principals of Enron, Tyco, and WorldCom, Inc., in the late 1990s and early 2000s. Employees and other investors were robbed of billions of dollars by criminals employed as corporate executives, who personally pocketed monies through fraudulent conduct.

In the wake of corporate greed and transgressions, SOX was enacted to restore investor confidence in corporate governance. The multitude of corporate bankruptcies, conflicts of interest, and accounting scandals necessitated aggressive measures around accounting, financial reporting, and enforcement of accounting principles.

SOX creates new standards for corporate accountability, imposes new penalties for violations, and contains significant protections for corporate whistleblowers.

Unfair competition: Here are three major federal antitrust laws in effect today:

- Sherman Act

- Clayton Act

- Federal Trade Commission Act

The Sherman Act prohibits, among other things, all contracts, combinations, and conspiracies that unreasonably restrain trade. Those agreements can include price fixing, bid rigging, market division, customer allocation, and group boycotts. There is other conduct that may constitute a restraint of trade, depending on its economic impact.

The Sherman Act also prohibits monopolization, attempted monopolization, and conspiracies to monopolize. Absent the company having market power, which is often indicated by a high market share, concerns about an unlawful monopoly are remote. Yet, consider the litigation that recently erupted in the literary world.

In February 2013, three independent bookstores filed a lawsuit against Amazon and the six major publishers (i.e., Hachette, Penguin, Simon & Schuster, HarperCollins, Random House, and Macmillan) that control approximately 60 percent of the print book market. The bookstores claim that, by entering into secret agreements, Amazon and the publishers seek to create a monopoly by controlling the digital restrictions management status of e-books, which prevents them from being shared on any e-reader device.[45]

The second major antitrust law is the Clayton Act, which prohibits, among other things, mergers and acquisitions that operate to substantially lessen competition or tend to create a monopoly.

The third law is the Federal Trade Commission Act, which is the statute used by the Federal Trade Commission to enforce civil antitrust violations. A violation of the Sherman Act or Clayton Act would typically result in liability under the Federal Trade Commission Act.

In a competitive global economy, there is a possibility that you'll be employed by a company that conducts business within and outside the borders of the United States. You may even be hired to work in a foreign country as an employee of a U.S. company.

The Foreign Corrupt Practices Act (FCPA) is a statute that, among other things:

- Prohibits the bribery of foreign officials;

- Imposes certain accounting requirements for companies whose securities are listed in the United States;

- Applies to all individuals and public or private companies in the United States, foreign nationals, and companies with the required connection to the United States; and

- Imposes severe sanctions for statutory violations.

The FCPA is currently enforced vigorously and includes two components:

1. Anti-bribery provisions, which criminalize the bribery of a foreign official to obtain or retain business; and

2. Recordkeeping and accounting provisions, which require that companies whose securities are listed in the United States maintain accurate books and records and an effective system of internal controls.[46]

The key elements of the anti-bribery provisions make it unlawful for a U.S. citizen, a U.S. company, or any other person in the United States with corrupt intent to offer, pay, promise to pay, or authorize payment of, directly or indirectly, anything of value to:

- A "foreign official," foreign political party (or official thereof), or any candidate for foreign political office (each a "covered official")

- Any person while "knowing" that all or a portion of the payment or thing of value will be offered, given, or promised directly or indirectly to a covered official:

  - For the purpose of influencing any official act or decision, inducing any act or omission in violation of a lawful official duty, or securing an improper advantage; and/or

  - In order to assist in obtaining or retaining business, or directing business to any person or firm.

"Anything of value" is broadly defined to include:

- Gifts

- Entertainment, meals, and travel expenses

- Incentive payments

- Free products, samples, discounts, donations

- Employment

- Consultancies

- Charitable contributions

Examples of potential violations include:

- Bribing a judge to make a case "go away"

- Bribing an official to win a contract

- Paying a scientist in a state-owned laboratory or company to buy your product

- Paying a customs official to allow a shipment of your product into a country without the proper permit or license

- Taking a foreign official to an extravagant dinner

- Helping a relative of a foreign official get a lucrative job

- Making a donation to a foreign official's favorite charity

- Taking a foreign official to lunch to discuss potential business ventures and recording the expense as a "licensing fee" on your records

Please note that these and other laws are aggressively enforced to fight illegal activities, including laws that prohibit false statements to federal agencies, perjury, obstruction of justice, conspiracies to defraud the United States, and mail and wire fraud. Many of these crimes carry their own fines and imprisonment terms, which may be added to the fines and imprisonment terms for antitrust law violations.[47]

Frequently raised employment laws: Most federal and state employment laws were passed decades ago, but they change often, either through legislation or legal decisions.

The following are federal laws:

The U.S. Equal Employment Opportunity Commission (EEOC) is the federal law enforcement agency that:

- Enforces laws against workplace discrimination;

- Investigates discrimination complaints based on an individual's race, color, national origin, religion, sex, age, disability, genetic information, and retaliation for reporting, participating in, and/or opposing a discriminatory practice;

- Mediates and settles thousands of discrimination complaints each year;

- Is empowered to file discrimination suits against employers on behalf of alleged victims; and

- Is empowered to adjudicate claims of discrimination brought against federal agencies.

Civil Rights Act of 1964 (Title VII) prohibits discrimination (including harassment and retaliation) because of race, color, sex, religion, and national origin. Harassment is a form of discrimination that has received a considerable share of attention.

There are two types of harassment:

1. ***Quid pro quo***—unwelcome sexual advances, requests for sexual favors, and other verbal or physical conduct of a sexual nature

2. ***Hostile work environment***—behavior that alters the terms, conditions, and/or reasonable expectations of a comfortable work environment, or behavior that is discriminatory in nature

The victim and the harasser can be male or female, and the victim and harasser can be the same gender. Harassment doesn't have to be of a sexual nature, however, and can include offensive remarks about a person's gender, race, ethnicity, religion, or other protected class.

For example, it's illegal to harass:

- A woman, by making offensive comments about women in general; or

- Catholics, Baptists, Muslims, or members of any other religion because of their religious practices and observances.

The harasser can be the victim's supervisor, a supervisor in another area, a coworker, or someone who isn't an employee of the employer, such as a client or customer.

Pregnancy Discrimination Act of 1964 forbids discrimination based on pregnancy when it comes to any aspect of employment, including hiring, firing, pay, job assignments, promotions, layoff, training, fringe benefits (e.g., leave and health insurance), and any other term or condition of employment.

Age Discrimination in Employment Act (ADEA) prohibits discrimination against individuals aged forty and over. There is also an **Older Workers Benefits Protection Act (OWBPA)**, which was passed by Congress in 1990 as an amendment to the ADEA to safeguard the employee benefits of older workers from age discrimination.

Americans with Disabilities Act of 1990 (ADA) prohibits discrimination against individuals with physical or mental disabilities. This act requires an employer to provide reasonable accommodation to qualified individuals with disabilities who are employees or applicants for employment, unless to do so would cause undue hardship.

Americans with Disabilities Act Amendments Act (ADAAA) expanded the definition of a disability to make it easier to prove that someone is disabled. It added new "major life activities," including eating, sleeping, bending, reading, concentrating, thinking, communicating, and major bodily functions.

Fair Labor Standards Act (FLSA) establishes minimum wage, overtime pay, recordkeeping, and youth-employment standards affecting employees in the private sector and in federal, state, and local governments. It provides that nonexempt workers are entitled to a minimum wage of not less than $7.25 per hour, effective July 24, 2009. Individual state wage and hour laws may differ, and may be higher but not lower than the federal minimum wage.

Under the FLSA, overtime pay at a rate not less than one and one-half times the regular rate of pay is required after forty hours of work in a workweek. State wage and hour laws may require the payment of overtime on the basis of the number of hours worked daily.

For example, a state law may provide that employees who work more than eight hours a day will be paid time and one-half (one and one-half times the regular rate of pay) for the hours worked in excess of eight hours. In that case, if employees work ten hours in a day, they would receive two hours of overtime pay.

Equal Pay Act of 1963 (EPA) prohibits gender-based discrimination in compensation for equal work, which means that all things being equal, such as experience and education, men and women must receive the same compensation if they perform the same job.

Lilly Ledbetter Fair Pay Act of 2009 allows pay-discrimination claims to be filed within 180/300 days of the issuance of the discriminatory paycheck.

Family & Medical Leave Act (FMLA) requires covered employers to provide twelve weeks of job-protected, unpaid leave to eligible employees for qualifying events, such as a serious personal illness or the serious illness of a spouse, child, or parent. An employee who is eligible to receive an FMLA leave is entitled to the leave, even if it poses some hardship to the company.

Fair Credit Reporting Act (FCRA) is designed to promote accuracy, fairness, and privacy of information in the files of every "consumer reporting agency." This means that access to the files of applicants for employment is limited. Consent is also required for reports that are provided to employers, or reports that contain medical information.

Candidates:

■ Can find out what is in their file;

■ Must be told if information in their report has been used against them;

■ Have a fair opportunity to dispute any errors or resolve issues they may never have known about; and

■ Can request that inaccurate information be corrected or deleted.

Remember the "when you hear hoofbeats in the hallway, think horses, not zebras"[48] quote if you believe that you're the victim of employment discrimination or retaliation because you exercised your legal rights under a federal or state law. Perhaps there is a simple, more common, and less reprehensible explanation for your situation.

For example, if you weren't selected for the job or promotion, ask yourself whether you've been the best employee you could be. Look around and ask yourself whether there are other employees who work harder and have better skills.

Don't rely on your length of service to justify a promotion. Unless a collective bargaining agreement provision or company policy provides otherwise, length of service simply does not carry the weight it did years ago.

Occupational Safety & Health Administration (OSHA) is the agency responsible for establishing health and safety standards and rules under the Occupational Safety & Health Act to prevent injuries and death in the workplace.

Health Insurance Portability and Accountability Act of 1996 (HIPAA) provides federal protections for personal health information held by covered entities and gives patients an array of rights with respect to that information.

ETHICS

Ethical considerations typically involve the moral tension between right and wrong.

Employees should be aware that moral compasses differ from person to person and from business to business. Consequently, as an employee, it's in your best interest to keep abreast of your employer's public persona and reputation.

As discussed earlier, the definition of ethics might vary from person to person, but the inquiry into the moral judgment about right or good is at the heart of the analysis.

Business ethics also focus on what is right, fair, and just in the business world based on decisions made by employees at all levels in the course of their daily activities in the workplace.

Although unethical conduct doesn't always result in an illegal act, it may be a fine line. For example, a salesman submits a large order for merchandise to a customer who he knows is near bankruptcy and who likely won't be able to pay for the merchandise. The salesman also knows that, by the time his sales manager confirms that the customer won't pay, the salesman will have received his commission, credits toward the annual "most productive sales people" trip to St. Barts, and any other quarterly prizes or recognition given for the highest sales. You see, the salesman plans to leave the company immediately after he returns from St. Barts.

The salesman's conduct may not be illegal, but it's certainly unethical. Of course, your objective is to stay out of an orange jumpsuit, the garment worn by inmates in penitentiaries. However, avoiding the taint associated with unethical behavior is just as important to your reputation and personal brand, and to your goals of achieving success and being respected.

CHAPTER TEN

Letter to Veterans

Dear Veterans:

First and foremost, thank you for your service to our country. One of the biggest advantages you have as veterans in a very competitive job market is that your countrymen and women are sincerely grateful to you for your contribution to our national security.

As you begin to look for work, take a deep breath and prepare yourself for the task ahead. You should set reasonable expectations, so you don't become discouraged if you don't find a job immediately.

There are so many ways people can help you if you don't limit yourself to contacting people through social media. Online networking is a critical element of the job-search dynamic, but don't underestimate the value of face-to-face contact.

People can introduce you to other people, who will introduce you to other people. Someone may be an HR representative, who can

Artwork by LYMAN DALLY

review your résumé and give you feedback. Someone else may know someone else who has an open position. The possibilities are endless, but it takes time, patience, and perseverance, and you have to let people know that you need and want help.

As you search for employment, it's important to gather information about where job opportunities are and the businesses that are hiring. Walmart has pledged to hire 100,000 veterans over the next five years, beginning on Memorial Day 2013. This new hiring program is open only to veterans who have left active-duty service in the prior twelve-month period. http://www.huffingtonpost.com/2013/01/15/walmart-hire-veterans

Incorporate the reasons to hire veterans identified in the articles on these websites in your introductory e-mails, cover letters, marketing pitch, résumés, and thank-you communications. http://www.veteranstoday.com/2010/01/25/10-top-reasons-to-hire-veterans/ and http://www.hireheroesusa.org/hire-a-veteran/why-hire-a-veteran/

For example, in your marketing pitch, begin by extending your hand and offering a firm handshake. Smile, and then start by saying the following:

> Hello, I'm _____. I'm returning to civilian life after ___ years in the military [or identify the branch of the armed services]. My demonstrated ability to learn new skills and concepts resulted in my selection to become an assistant instructor eighteen months after I joined the service.
>
> Subsequently, I was also selected by my peers to lead our team's community service initiative (or team effort) to_____. My security clearances speak to my integrity and trustworthiness.
>
> I'd welcome any guidance and input you can give me about my future employment possibilities and opportunities.

Communication is an essential job-search skill. Like non-English-speaking civilians who are looking for employment, veterans have to translate their military skills, experience, and training in order to communicate to human resource and hiring managers that they meet the job requirements.

The following links will help you "de-jargon" or reword military terms and better communicate what you can bring to the table and the value you can add to an organization. "Employing America's Veterans Perspectives from Businesses 2012."[49] http://www.cnas.org/employingamericasveterans, pp. 21-23; https://www.usaa.com/inet/pages/usaamag_job_front; http://www.military.com/veteran-jobs/skills-translator/

One thing to keep in mind in your oral and written communications and interactions are employers' perceptions about veterans. Some of the common favorable perceptions are that you:

- Play by the rules because the military requires compliance, and there are consequences if rules are not followed;

- Respect and honor the chain of command, and believe that superior officers are due respect and orders should be obeyed;

- Are a team player and loyal to your compatriots;

- Are mission-directed and therefore trained to be goal-oriented (i.e., you stay the course, unless ordered to do otherwise, until the mission is achieved); and

- Have a neat, buttoned-up appearance.

Additional favorable perceptions may be found in the following article and websites: "Employing America's Veterans Perspectives from Businesses 2012," pp. 15, 17-20, http://www.cnas.org/employingamericasveterans; http://www.veteranstoday.com/2010/01/25/10-top-reasons-to-hire-veterans/

Although you should focus on the favorable perceptions, be aware that there are also less favorable perceptions. Here are a few:

- Your reluctance to question authority may not translate to civilian life.

  ☐ Unsolicited feedback and input are generally encouraged and expected in civilian workplaces.

☐   Promotional opportunities are more plentiful and are handled more systematically in the military.

■   You're not used to keen competition and the more competitive environment found in many workplaces.

■   You may miss the camaraderie you enjoyed in the military. Esprit de corps (e.g., the common spirit existing among the members of a group and inspiring enthusiasm, devotion, and strong regard for the honor of the group) may look different from what you expect.

Additional less favorable perceptions can be found on pp. 21-29 of "Employing America's Veterans Perspectives from Businesses 2012." http://www.cnas.org/employingamericasveterans

Now that you know some of the challenges in terms of perception, do your best to present yourself in a manner that highlights the favorable ones.

You are military proud, as you should be, but your pride should not get in the way of the networking you will have to do to maximize your ability to find a job. Remember, whatever the perception, your formal military training, ability to perform under pressure, and security clearances make you an attractive candidate for employment.

I leave you with this thought: You are already desirable candidates because of your training, your professional appearance, your respect for authority, and your can-do/will-do attitude. Spend as much time daily looking for a job as you would if you were working, and you'll find the job opportunity you're looking for. After you find that job, rely on your military training and experience to achieve success.

Again, thank you for your service to our country, and good luck to you all.

Sincerest regards,

CHAPTER ELEVEN

Lights, Cameras, Action

Personal Considerations

I, not events, have the power to make me happy or unhappy. Today, I can choose which it shall be.

—Groucho Marx (1890–1977), American comedian, film, and television star

112 Think of the employment experience as a film production.

Each phase of your employment life will require that you project an image that translates into success. Depending on your personality and your life experience to date, in order to be successful, you may have to step outside your comfort zone.

If you're shy, reticent, and soft spoken, you will need to call upon your inner being to help you project an image that differs from the person you may be. If you are an extrovert with an exuberant, bubbly personality, you may have to dial it back.

The challenge is to strike a balance, which results in a persona that employment decision makers find appealing; unfortunately, what constitutes a balance may change from interview to interview, and from employer to employer.

One way to think of your employment experience is to envision it as the production of a film.

- Always remember that the employer is the "money man" or the producer of the film.

- Never underestimate the power that the producer has over the production of the film.

- As the director (as least over your performance) and an actor in the film, you, too, have power.

- Your objective as both actor and director is to give and get the best performance possible.

- As the director, you decide the role you will play: star, supporting actor, or extra.

- You're acutely aware that the producer may decide that you are well suited for roles in which you have no interest.

- The producer may also decide that you are not suited for bigger roles.

- Recognize that there is an inherent bias or conflict of interest when "directors" evaluate their own performance.

- Recognize that, because you lack objectivity, your assessment of your performance may not be sound or reliable, especially if the producer's assessment is inconsistent with yours.

- If you don't feel that your contribution to the film is valued, or if you do not feel it's the right role for you, leave the film.

- Generally, you should not leave one role unless you're sure you have another one.

- You know or should know your circumstances better than anyone else.

The decision is yours.

Don't get it twisted: Stay grounded. The film-production analogy isn't an invitation for you to go "Hollywood." Diva-like behavior and thinking that you're the next Beyoncé, Blake Lively, Robert Pattinson, or Lenny Kravitz are unacceptable.

It's your decision whether to remain in the role or leave when you have found another producer (employer), who appears to appreciate your talents and offers you a better opportunity. Your decision shouldn't be made in the heat of anger or without well-reasoned reflection.

113 Strike a balance between your work responsibilities and your home life.

Don't work to the exclusion of everything and everyone else. Success at work will enable you to be independent and enjoy some of the pleasures of life. If you work too many hours each day, every day, you'll miss the many pleasures and events that motivate you. Make sure to stop and smell the flowers.

Don't get it twisted: Don't tell your supervisor that you've worked enough for one week. If you're an hourly employee, there may be scheduled and unscheduled overtime. Salaried employees may work more hours without additional pay. When there are deadlines or unexpected situations that require you to work longer hours, do what's necessary to get the job done.

114 Give back by making charitable donations and/or donating your time.

Whatever good you do comes back to you. Giving of yourself and your time is rewarding on many levels. Don't forget those less fortunate because a change in circumstances could find you in their place.

Volunteer ... help others less fortunate.

115 If life gives you lemons, make lemonade.

116 Be prepared to do the work necessary
to achieve your goal.

Most successful people who have achieved the career and life goals they
set for themselves are usually willing to share with others what they
learned along the way, especially those just beginning the journey.

- You understand that the journey will likely test your resilience and self-confidence.

- You should remember always that "you have the freedom to pull the superstar out of yourself"[50] to become the superstar you were born to be.

- You must be prepared to do the work to achieve success.

If life gives you lemons, turn them into lemonade. Turn a negative into a positive. Consider some of Jay-Z's life lessons:

- Never fear the truth.

- The work you put in will be what you get out.

- Believe in and be true to yourself.

- Bring your best.

- Learn from your failures as well as your successes.

- Stand for something.

- Have integrity and honor.

- Learn how to let go so you can move on.[51]

Learn more about the successful people you respect and want to emulate by reading whatever you can find about their climb to success, remembering always that success is defined differently by different people. Again, the Internet is a treasure trove of useful information.

You can achieve your goals if you do the work, providing your goals are:

- Realistic

- Reasonable

■   Attainable given your skillset, experience, education, personality, and work ethic

Remember the picture in the frame that you placed on your desk or by your bedside? Tell yourself, "I can do anything. I can achieve anything that I put my mind to if I work hard and meet the requirements identified." *It's the truth.*

Before you begin your employment journey, either to get hired or be promoted, be sure that you've done all the work necessary to move onward and upward.

If you have, then lights, camera, action—it's time for you to star in your chosen career.

117   Before you begin each day, remember that whether or not you will be happy is your choice.

118   Don't let anyone make that choice for you or steal your joy.

> *No matter what your history has been, your destiny is what you create today. What are you going to create?*
>
> —Steve Maraboli, speaker, author, personal coach, and national radio show host

Rely on yourself to set your course and navigate the employment terrain. Don't expect your job search and subsequent success on the job to be a priority with anyone else, including your loved ones. It's not that they don't care or aren't interested. They simply have their own concerns and interests.

Never be afraid to be your own cheerleader. There is nothing to be ashamed of if you set goals for yourself, create a plan, execute your plan, and take pride in your accomplishments. Once you achieve success as you define it, take time to enjoy it. *You deserve it!*

Believe you can and you're halfway there.

Theodore Roosevelt, twenty-sixth
President of the United States

GET THE JOB

Done ✔

Career Toolkit

118 Career Tips, Tools, and Internet Resources

Tips

1. Get advice from people you respect and who are knowledgeable.

2. Follow sound advice unless you have a good reason not to do so.

3. Manage your expectations.

4. Make sure your expectations are realistic.

5. You don't know what you don't know and why you don't know it.

6. Seek information, not affirmation.

7. To your loved ones, you may be all that and a bag of chips but, in the workplace, you're an employee and a coworker.

8. Your family members aren't always right, but they're not always wrong.

9. Select and maintain relationships thoughtfully and wisely.

10. You can dress, talk, and conduct yourself as you choose, but be prepared to accept the consequences.

11. Don't hate the player; hate the game.

12. Consider all feedback a gift, and learn to accept negative feedback without becoming defensive.

13. Don't shoot the messenger.

14. Have a positive attitude.

15. You're not better than anyone else, and no one is better than you are.

16. Accept that there is a New Employment Reality, and embrace it.

17. "Job security" is a contradiction in terms.

18. Your employment matters are solely your responsibility.

19. Acquiring a job is a competition.

20. Finding a job in the New Employment Reality requires work.

21. Consider relocating to other states and countries to find employment.

22. Be flexible about changing jobs and employers.

23. Keep your career goals and objectives fluid.

24. Acquire more training, including a bachelor's degree (if you don't have one) or a graduate degree (if you have an undergraduate one) to expand your skillset.

25. Identify ways to create additional income streams.

26. Understand that, generally, it's your employer's party and you're an invited guest.

27. Don't let it happen; make it happen.

28. Understand, accept, and brace yourself for a drain on your energy.

29. Realize that you have a limited amount of energy and time to devote to the number of tasks you have to fit into a twenty-four-hour day.

30. Get into the right state of mind and remain focused.

31. Train like an athlete because you'll need endurance and strength on your employment journey.

32. Motivate yourself.

33. Stay in shape or get in shape. (Consult a physician before you begin any fitness program.)

34. Take a break ... be kind to yourself!

35. Don't give up or give in.

36. Use social media wisely.

37. Don't engage in conduct that you wouldn't want your loved ones to view in any form of media, including social-networking sites.

38. Consider the possible long-term consequences before you post material on social-networking sites.

39. If you "friend" a coworker, be sure not to post anything that might be used against you to damage your reputation at work.

40. It's a high-tech world, but don't forget the human factor.

41. Tell everyone you know, and anyone you meet but don't know, that you're looking for a job and you need their help.

42. Acknowledge perceptions about your strengths and weaknesses.

43. By your conduct, refute negative perceptions.

44. Strive to establish a reputation as a person who is hard working, detail oriented, honest, ethical, reliable, punctual, polite, and a team player.

45. View yourself as a professional.

46. By your conduct, create that impression so that others view you likewise.

47. Embrace differences.

48. Learn from people who are different.

49. Overcome prejudice and biases.

50. Avoid discussions about religion, politics, sex, health problems, problems with loved ones, and your career aspirations.

51. Don't let your ego get in the way. If you don't know, say so.

52. Your clothes shouldn't enter the room before you do because you're more important than your clothes.

53. Before you leave for work or for an interview, look in the mirror and ask yourself, "Is this the statement I want to make?"

54. Don't be fooled by workplace dress codes that permit "business casual" or "dress-down" days.

55. Emulate the style of dress that is common at the level of the position you aspire to achieve.

56. Don't forget to master the social graces.

57. Always treat people the way you want to be treated and require the same from others.

58. Be courteous, pleasant, and helpful to everyone, including administrative assistants and other support staff.

59. Practice cell phone and texting etiquette.

60. Conduct a self-assessment.

61. Develop a plan and execute it.

62. Remember: There is nothing like the prospect of success and prosperity.

63. Whether you're employed or unemployed, attention to detail is essential.

64. Seek employment with employers who encourage and value ethics and integrity.

65. If you have a disability, decide when or whether to disclose it.

66. Don't appear desperate when interviewing for a job.

67. Seriously consider a temporary position.

68. Looking for a job takes work (e.g., time, effort, focus, and follow-up).

69. Résumés must be complete, concise, accurate, neat, and easy to read.

70. Your résumé should contain key words and phrases that will help identify you as a potential candidate.

71. Include a cover letter with your résumé unless you're told not to do so.

72. Always, always send a thank-you note or e-mail following an interview.

73. Face background-check problems head on.

74. If you are fortunate enough to have more than one offer, notify other employers that you have accepted another offer.

75. Negotiate your compensation package strategically.

76. Your success on the job depends on you.

77. Be the best employee you can be.

78. Take or make opportunities to discuss the company with more senior employees.

79. You're not better than anyone else, and no one is better than you are.

80. Authority is not always handled well by everyone who has it.

81. Respect authority and the chain of command.

82. When possible, avoid toxic people.

83. Don't let anyone diminish your self-esteem.

84. Continue to research your employer after you're hired.

85. Look for creative ways to position yourself, so that your potential is recognized.

86. Learn your employer's abbreviations, language, and business culture.

87. If you pay attention, people will show their true colors. When they do, reassess your opinion of and your relationship with them; you may regret it if you don't.

88. Make your supervisor look good.

89. Don't try to teach your supervisor that you have a better style; it usually doesn't work.

90. If you have one approach and your supervisor has another, it's recommended that you change.

91. Don't overcommit and underdeliver.

92. Don't presume that you're performing well on the job if you haven't been told so, and your performance reviews don't confirm that you are.

93. If you have a problem with your supervisor or a coworker, assume good intentions unless and until you confirm that your assumption is incorrect.

94. Cultivate a respectful relationship with coworkers at all levels in the organization and with clients.

95. Help others reach their goals.

96. Connect with new people in the organization.

97. Provide constructive criticism in a way that will make people seek your input.

98. Feedback should be given in a tactful, diplomatic manner.

99. Find a knowledgeable mentor and/or hire a career coach.

100. Don't share your personal business in the workplace.

101. Don't expect or look for love at work.

102. Keep your loved ones out of the workplace.

103. Don't sh*t where you eat.

104. Don't engage in criminal, unethical, or otherwise unprofessional behavior on or off the job.

105. At work, the only place you should expect privacy is behind the locked door of a bathroom stall.

106. Continue to conduct periodic self-assessments.

107. Loyalty and trust are important but not always reciprocated.

108. After you become employed, maintain the contacts you made and the network you developed during your job search because you never know when you may need them again.

109. If you can't take it anymore, find another job before you resign.

110. Take advantage of your employer's benefits.

111. If your employer has an employee assistance program, check it out. You may not need it now, but you may need it later.

112. Think of the employment experience as a film production.

113. Strike a balance between your work responsibilities and your home life.

114. Give back by making charitable donations and/or donating your time.

115. If life gives you lemons, make lemonade.

116. Be prepared to do the work necessary to achieve your goal.

117. Before you begin each day, remember that whether or not you will be happy is your choice.

118. Don't let anyone make that choice for you or steal your joy.

Workplace Words and Phrases

- "Hold your powder" or "Keep your powder dry" (as in gun powder) means "Be quiet. Don't assert your position or take a different position from the group."

- "That dog won't/don't hunt" means "That is not a good idea."

- "Think outside the box" means "Be more creative and less traditional."

- "I don't have a nickel in that dime," "I don't have a dog in that fight," or "I don't have any skin in the game" means "I don't have any interest or involvement in the situation."

- "Chum in the water" means "to incite competition among employees" or "a feeding frenzy."

- "Drill down" means "a comprehensive, thorough review or approach," including details.

- "Granular" means "detailed."

- "Get your hands dirty" means "No matter how big or small the task, do whatever is necessary to get the job done."

- "Is that the hill you want to die on?" means "Are you sure you want to take that position or make that argument?"

- An "elevator speech" is a 90-second, oral, self-promotional marketing pitch.

- "Brand loyalty" means that you're not easily lured away from a particular product.

- "He/she doesn't make me reach for my wallet" means "I'm not impressed."

- "He/she is an A, B, or C player," where A=Excellent, B=Good, and C=Average.

- "He/she has runway" means "He/she has the ability and enough years left, is junior enough to be of service for a long time, or has enough years left in his/her career to be of service."

- "Drank the Kool-Aid" means "accepted the company line despite evidence that there is something wrong or unethical."

- "Don't write a check you can't cash" means "Don't start something you can't finish."

- If your boss says, "I'm done" or "I've had or heard enough," it's time to stop talking.

- "On the same page" means "in agreement."

- If you hear, "I don't disagree," *be careful* because this sentence is ambiguous. It isn't absolute agreement. It doesn't say, "I agree." Two negatives equal a positive, but it's risky to assume complete agreement.

- "Hits the ground running" means "The person is a self-starter and needs little supervision."

- "Add value" means "Be an asset to the business."

- "Don't bring a slingshot to a gunfight" means "If you take on an unpopular or opposing side, bring everything you've got, and be prepared to defend your position."

- "Throw a person under the bus" or "Put someone on Front Street" means "Disclose information that will have adverse consequences for someone or cast him/her in a negative light."

■   An "800-pound gorilla" is "a person, usually an executive or a client, who generates a lot of revenue for the company or has a great deal of influence."

■   "Tough times don't last; tough people do" means "Hard, tough times will always come and go but, when tough-minded people hit a rough patch, they persevere and get through the tough times."

■   "It's better to have and not need than to need and not have" means "Be prepared."

■   "That's good feedback" means "Thanks for your input."

■   An "elephant in the room" is a subject or situation that people know about but, for some reason, are uncomfortable discussing.

■   A "stretch assignment" requires an employee to work outside his/her comfort zone by challenging current skills while acquiring new or additional skills.

■   "Soft skills" are social traits, such as personality, friendliness, helpfulness, and integrity.

■   To "micromanage" means to "supervise with excessive control or attention to minute details." This management style has a negative connotation.

■   "Pink-collar jobs" are traditionally filled by women.

■   "360-degree feedback" is an evaluation tool, which requires the collection of information about an individual manager's work performance from a variety of knowledgeable sources and stakeholders, including subordinates, peers, and customers, his/her direct supervisor, and a self-assessment by the manager. http://www.ehow.com/about_5125338_degree-evaluation.html#ixzz2ZuMQ83Oz

Marketing Pitch

(Old-School & New-School) Networking
is the GPS to Employment Success®

Today, there is a heightened intensity that accompanies job searches because of the seismic shift in the employment landscape. Each day, a tremendous number of people vie for an ever more limited number of job openings.

Consequently, anyone who is looking for work should use all available resources aggressively and exhaustively because the great lead that results in a great job can come from anywhere.

Objective: To include all possible strategies and advantages in your job-search arsenal. You may be surprised by the number of people you know, and how extensive your networks are when you tap into them.

Preparation: Maximize the likelihood of favorable job-search results by embracing both new-school and old-school networking. Both methods should be used simultaneously and vigorously. To use an old-school phrase, "Leave no stone unturned."

New-school networking favors the speed of more impersonal electronic connections and submissions and social networks to share information and communicate thoughts, ideas, hopes, and dreams. Social media is a great tool. Unquestionably, electronic tablets, laptops, smartphones, and various types of social media are useful devices and essential to achieving employment success; however, it is foolhardy to rely on them exclusively or even primarily.

By all means, use Facebook, Twitter, texting, and any other form of social media and communication that connects you with people and allows you to tell them that you need their help to find a job.

Friends and other contacts may look you up on Facebook or LinkedIn or search Google before they refer you. Consequently, you want to make sure that you do not have anything on social media sites that hampers your efforts to find a job.

Old-school networking is person-to-person contact, especially referrals and recommendations. This approach can almost magically get a person in the door for at least an exploratory interview.

The reason: Given the number of talented, educated, skilled people looking for work, hiring decisions will be made based in part on intangibles, on first impressions based on personal appearance, and on the prospective employee's ability to communicate. Who knows whom, who referred whom, who is related to whom, who owes whom a favor, and who wants to make points with the person who made the referral may also be factors in hiring decisions.

Prepare a brief (no longer than 90-second) marketing pitch, which is:

- A self-serving, self-focused commercial; and

- An opportunity to highlight your attributes, such as verbal skills, poise, presence, and personality.

The pitch should have the following key points:

- Your experience, strengths, and accomplishments

- The type of work or position you are seeking

- Why you are interested in that type of work or industry

- Why you are attending the event or what you are seeking (optional)

Sample Content

If you're a recent college graduate and you're looking for your first job:

- Identify clubs in which you've participated and the contributions you have made (e.g., teams, hobbies, scouts, cheerleading, theatre, soccer, tennis, sports, and leadership roles).

- If you're a member of a team or participate in sports, list the attributes (e.g., focus, practice, reliability, and teamwork) that contributed to successful results for the team.

- List experiences you've had that have contributed to your personal development (e.g., when you were a lifeguard, you were, among other things, reliable and trustworthy, and you paid attention to details).

If you've been out of the workforce for a while:

- Identify leadership roles (if any) and activities in which you've participated and the contributions you've made.

- Identify the skills that made you effective as a volunteer, parent, or caregiver.

Sample Marketing Pitches

- "Hello, I'm_____. It's nice to meet you. I just (graduated from/received a certificate or diploma from/completed training at) _____, where I (majored in/specialized in/focused on) _____."

- "As a member of the _____ (team/group/chorus/organization) in (college/high school/my community/my religious group), I contributed to the success of (identify the project/ the effort/the event)."

■ "As a volunteer at _____, I increased the number of clients we were able to serve by streamlining our enrollment process."

■ "I'm proficient in Microsoft Office and other frequently used computer software programs. My computer skills have been described as impressive."

■ "Anyone who knows me will tell you that I'm a reliable, hard worker, who is strategic as well as tactical." (Be prepared to provide examples that illustrate how you were strategic and tactical.)

■ "I work well on a team, but I'm also a leader."

■ "I get the job done! I deliver."

■ "I go the extra mile to provide a quality product."

■ "I can add value to your team or organization by working hard, being punctual, and paying addition to detail."

■ "I'm willing to jump in to fill any void on the team."

■ "I want to be your 'go-to' person."

■ "My personal brand is best described in two words: hard worker."

Personal Marketing Plan

How to Market Yourself

Once again, given the number of talented, educated, skilled people who are looking for work, hiring decisions made in the worst economy since the Great Depression will be made based in part on intangibles. Remember the importance of first impressions. You need a plan.

- Adopt a positive yet realistic state of mind.

- Conduct a self-assessment where you highlight strengths and improve weaknesses.

- Prepare and practice your marketing pitch.

- Research industries and businesses that interest you and to which you think you can make a contribution.

- Learn about the personal appearance required for those businesses and decide whether it fits you.

- Identify events where you'll meet people.

- Check various media outlets for possibilities.

- Prepare:

  - ☐ Cover letters, résumés, thank-you letters, business cards, and e-mails (with no typographical errors!);

  - ☐ Voicemail greetings;

  - ☐ E-mail addresses; and

☐ Introductions.

■ Learn the power of networking in the following ways:

☐ Use the "Job Search Networking Log" on the next page.

☐ Prepare a contact list all the people you know.

☐ Create a database.

☐ Back up all job-search material on an external hard drive.

☐ Attend events and meetings where you'll meet people who may be able to help you.

☐ Thank all contacts who do anything to help you.

■ Learn the power of social media in the following ways:

☐ Evaluate your digital footprint.

☐ Check and recheck your social media presence.

☐ If you can't erase negative digital material, create a brief, honest talk track to explain.

■ Use the "Before-You-Leave-for-the-Interview Checklist" to make sure that your appearance conveys the message you want to send when you attend networking events or interviews.

■ Practice, practice, practice.

■ Take a break periodically.

Job Search Networking Log

Name	Title	Contact Information	Referred By	Met at an Event	Date of Contact	Follow-up Dates

Date _____

Career Plan

Goal: ....

Target Date of Achievement: ....

Requirements: ....

....

....

Research Needed: ....

....

....

Additional Education Needed: ....

....

....

Additional Training Needed: ....

....

....

Networking Activities: ....

....

....

....

....

....

Status after One Year: ....

Status after 18 Months: ....

Status after Two Years: ....

Before-You-Leave-for-the-Interview Checklist

- Personal hygiene

  - ☐ Bring a mirror.

  - ☐ Shower/bathe; use deodorant/antiperspirant.

  - ☐ Use perfume/aftershave sparingly or not at all.

  - ☐ Get a clean, neat hairstyle or haircut.

  - ☐ Freshen breath and clean teeth free of food particles.

  - ☐ Have clean, neat nails; avoid anything that draws attention to your nails and is a distraction.

  - ☐ Shave, if you are a man. If you choose to retain facial hair, trim it.

  - ☐ Remove leg/nose/knuckle hair, and any other unflattering visual body hair.

  - ☐ Use moisturizer or lotion for a healthy, well-groomed look.

  - ☐ Check nose for cleanliness and eyes for cleanliness, and eliminate redness with eye drops.

- Clothing and Makeup—Women

  - ☐ Wear clean, pressed clothing that fits comfortably in either dark, neutral, or understated colors.

- ☐ If you wear makeup, aim for a natural, effortless look. Limit eye shadow and blush. Avoid vibrant lipstick shades.

- ☐ If you wear jewelry, avoid large earrings, and limit the number of pieces of jewelry worn at the same time.

- ☐ Your shoes (or boots, if inclement or very cold weather or snow) should be polished and in good shape. Make a trip to the shoe-repair shop, and avoid anything that draws attention to your shoes and is a distraction.

- ☐ Pantyhose/stockings/tights should be clean, with no runs, patterns or decorations.

- ■ Clothing—Men

  - ☐ Your suit or sports jacket should be clean, pressed, and fit correctly.

  - ☐ Select a white, blue, or pale yellow shirt with a tie.

  - ☐ Your slacks should be crisply ironed and in dark, neutral, or understated colors, worn at the waist with or without a belt, and fit comfortably. A belt should be worn if the slacks have belt loops.

  - ☐ Your shoes should be polished and in good shape. Make a trip to the shoe-repair shop, if necessary.

- ■ Unless you're applying to be a barista, chef, or professional athlete, cover tattoos and camouflage or remove body piercings.

- ■ Stand and sit erectly with your head up. Don't slouch or lean on your hand.

Interview Preparation Checklist

- Research the company and person or persons who will interview you (if you know or can find out).

- Practice your responses to questions on the interviewing websites provided in this toolkit as well as link your job skills and experience to the job requirements/qualifications provided in the job announcement.

- For telephone interviews:

  - ☐ Get up and dressed at least two hours before the interview.

  - ☐ Drink a hot beverage to clear your throat.

  - ☐ Stand up during the interview. Your voice is stronger this way.

  - ☐ Don't do anything during the telephone interview that you wouldn't do during an in-person interview. Remember that the person who used the bathroom during a telephone interview didn't get the job.

- Several days before the interview:

  - ☐ Research what is appropriate to wear to the interview:

    - ■ Have a friend contact HR to ask what applicants should wear.

- Ask someone you know who works there and who, because of his/her role with the business, has reliable information about the organization.

☐ Try on what you plan to wear to the interview to make sure that it is clean and pressed, fits, and you feel comfortable wearing it.

☐ Conduct a dry run to the interview location, ideally at the same time of day you will actually leave for the interview. You want to confirm that you know where to go, how to get there, where to park, and how much time it will take for you to arrive at the interview site with thirty minutes to spare.

■ On the day of the interview, bring the following items:

☐ Extra copies of your résumé, even if you've already e-mailed it to HR

☐ Business cards

☐ Work-related writing samples, artwork, etc.

☐ List of references, including contact information

☐ An umbrella, just in case it rains

☐ Tissues

☐ Tide to Go or Shout in individual packets because you may spill something on your outfit

☐ Emergency money

☐ Medication, if you take any

■ As soon as you arrive for the interview, go to the restroom to inspect your appearance, and pull yourself together visually and psychologically.

■ Remember to turn off your cell phone.

Now, take a deep breath, relax, and be confident. If you've done the work, you're ready for your interview.

Go get that job!

Resources

The links below will direct you to third-party websites that contain articles and blogs with job-search and career information. These websites represent only some of the content on the Internet.[52]

Take the time to explore these websites as well as other Internet sites for additional employment-related material. The comments also may be helpful to you. Only you can decide which information is suitable for you.

To access the information, visit www.youremploymentmatters. com or type (or copy and paste) the web address in the address bar of your browser. http://www.wikihow.com/Type-in-a-Web-Address-to-Go-to-a-Specific-Website.

Prepare for Your Job-Search Journey

The search for employment requires that you prepare yourself mentally, physically, and emotionally. Financial issues, rejection, and lack of response to or acknowledgement of résumés and telephone calls are results you may experience as you search for a job.

Books

Jack Canfield and Janet Switzer, *The Success Principles: How to Get from Where You Are to Where You Want to Be,* offers humorous, practical, and inspirational advice about how to be successful. http://www.barnesandnoble.com/w/success-principles-jack-l-canfield/1100553660?ean=9780007195084

Karen Reivich, *The Resilience Factor: 7 Keys to Finding Your Inner Strength and Overcoming Life's Hurdles,* offers seven techniques for improving an individual's ability to recover from setbacks. https://www.goodreads.com/book/show/1466276.The_Resilience_Factor

Al Siebert, PhD, *The Resiliency Advantage: Master Change, Thrive Under Pressure, and Bounce Back from Setbacks,* according to one description, helps readers banish negative, self-defeating thoughts and improve problem-solving skills. http://www.amazon.com/The-Resiliency-Advantage-Pressure-Setbacks/dp/1576753298

Maria Tabone, *The Holistic Root to Managing Anxiety,* provides a number of options for managing the stress and anxiety you will likely experience as you look for employment. http://www.amazon.com/The-Holistic-Root-Managing-Anxiety/dp/0615356222

Websites

http://www.oflikeminds.com/Unemployment.html

http://www.helpguide.org/life/unemployment_job_loss_stress_coping_tips.htm

http://ezinearticles.com/?Unemployed?-Tips-To-Go-From-Being-Unemployed-To-Employed&id=117695

http://www.theladders.com/career-advice/hot-topics/anxiety-depression-job-search

http://suite101.com/article/unemployment-job-loss-advice-a33739

http://careerspeed.com/articles/managing_finances_unemployed

http://exercise.about.com/od/healthinjuries/a/olympictraining.htm

Job Search 101

Books

Richard N. Bolles, *What Color is Your Parachute?,* is one of the first job-hunting books on the market, and one that is updated each year. After more than thirty years, it is considered by many to be the seminal job search/career resource. http://www.amazon.com/What-Color-Your-Parachute-2013/dp/1607741474

Ford R. Myers, *Get The Job You Want, Even When No One's Hiring: Take Charge of Your Career, Find a Job You Love, and Earn What You Deserve,* suggests strategies to land your dream job and claims to have a recession-proof plan to help you land that job. http://www.walmart.com/ip/Get-the-Job-You-Want-Even-When-No-One-s-Hiring-Take-Charge-of-Your-Career-Find-a-Job-You-Love-and-Earn-What-You-Deserve/10846221

Ellen Gordon Reeves, *Can I Wear My Nose Ring to the Interview? The Crash Course—Finding, Landing and Keeping Your First Job* is written by a résumé expert and covers, among other things, the do's and don'ts of résumé writing and cover letters. http://www.amazon.com/Can-Wear-Nose-Ring-Interview/dp/0761141456

Websites

http://jobs.aol.com/articles/2013/04/18/new-job-search-tips/

http://www.aarp.org/work/working-after-retirement/info-06-2011/jobs-for-a-second-career.html

http://www.cvtips.com/career_advice_forum/entries/489-Five-tips-for-job-hunting

http://www.huffingtonpost.com/2012/01/04/what-advice-do-you-have-for-job-searchers_n_1182015.html?utm_hp_ref=opportunity-working

Where Are the Jobs?

http://www.cvtips.com/career_advice_forum/entries/389-Stop-Applying-to-100-Jobs!

https://www.usajobs.gov/

http://jobs.aol.com/articles/2013/05/21/good-careers-high-school-degree-careercast/

http://www.aarp.org/work/working-after-retirement/info-06-2011/jobs-for-a-second-career.html

http://jobs.aol.com/articles/2013/03/05/high-demand-professional-certifications-programs/

http://jobs.aol.com/articles/2013/01/23/global-job-forecast-2013/

http://jobs.aol.com/articles/2013/03/03/in-demand-skills-find-job/

http://money.usnews.com/careers/best-jobs/rankings/the-100-best-jobs?s_cid=art_btm

http://www.nytimes.com/2013/03/07/business/economy/despite-job-vacancies-employers-shy-away-from-hiring.html?_r=0

http://jobs.aol.com/articles/top-10-companies-hiring/

http://jobs.aol.com/articles/2013/01/29/best-paying-college-majors/

http://jobs.aol.com/articles/2012/08/30/the-highest-paying-part-time-jobs-in-america/

http://www.salary.com/12-jobs-on-the-brink-will-they-evolve-or-go-extinct/slide/3/

http://jobs.aol.com/articles/2013/01/31/high-paying-jobs-that-dont-require-a-bachelors-degree/

http://jobs.aol.com/articles/2012/12/14/best-jobs-bachelors-degree-pay-benefits-2013/

http://www.thefiscaltimes.com/Articles/2012/01/12/The-10-Best-Cities-for-Young-People-to-Find-Jobs.aspx#page1

http://www.cvtips.com/career_advice_forum/entries/450-What-Jobs-are-in-Demand

http://www.ehow.com/how_5415404_control-job-hunt.html

http://www.cvtips.com/career_advice_forum/entries/389-Stop-Applying-to-100-Jobs!

http://www.ehow.com/how_4526418_job-todays-economy.html

http://www.badeconomyjobs.com/best-jobs/

http://exploredia.com/best-jobs-2013/

http://www.huffingtonpost.com/2012/06/13/creative-job-titles-jedis-ninjas-rock-stars-talent_n_1594539.html

http://www.thefiscaltimes.com/Media/Slideshow/2012/02/03/The-Fastest-Growing-Jobs-in-America

http://www.huffingtonpost.com/2012/06/21/health-care-job-creation_n_1613479.html?utm_hp_ref=careers

http://www.law.com/jsp/nj/PubArticleNJ.jsp?roi=echo4-21885433451-19588362-37e0a267dbec3f062d6cf563be176e24&id=1202586968705

http://www.thefiscaltimes.com/Media/Slideshow/2012/01/12/10-Best-Cities-for-Young-People-to-Find-Jobs

http://jobs.aol.com/articles/2013/03/03/dream-job-quiz/

http://www.huffingtonpost.com/arianna-huffington/millennials-stress_b_2718986.html?utm_source=DailyBrief&utm_campaign=022013&utm_medium=email&utm_content=FeatureTitle&utm_term=Daily%20Brief

http://www.huffingtonpost.com/2011/06/01/top-ten-cities-with-most-job-postings_n_869954.html

Popular Job Boards

http://jobsearch.about.com/od/joblistings/tp/jobbanks.htm is a link that connects to more than eight sites.

Career Assessments

http://www.quintcareers.com/career_assessment-dos-donts.html

http://www.quintcareers.com/online_career_assessments.html

http://www.careerpath.com/

http://careerplanning.about.com/cs/aboutassessment/a/assess_overview.htm

http://careerplanning.about.com/cs/aboutassessment/a/assess_overview.htm

http://www.onetonline.org/

http://www.buzzle.com/articles/personality-traits-list.html

http://www.ehow.com/list_6755299_list-vocational-careers.
html#ixzz2UWLLGRJ1

http://arizonanotebook.com/shortage-of-construction-workers-
projected-as-veteran-workers-begin-retiring

http://www.martindale.com/construction-law/article_Stites-
Harbison-PLLC_1745918.htm

http://rt.com/usa/plumbers-college-bloomberg-mayor-551/

http://www.constructionexec.com/Issues/April_2013/Features.aspx

http://www.forconstructionpros.com/press_release/10915670/
construction-jobs-reach-three-year-high-in-march-2013

http://careers.stateuniversity.com/pages/854/Vocational-Training.
html

Personal Branding

Books

Susan Chritton, *Personal Branding for Dummies,* offers advice about
how to create a professional presence and personal brand. http://
www.amazon.com/Personal-Branding-Dummies-Susan-Chritton/
dp/1118117921/ref=sr_1_1?s=books&ie=UTF8&qid=1369572219&
sr=1-1&keywords=personal+branding

Dorie Clark, *Reinventing You: Define Your Brand, Imagine
Your Future,* is a how-to-reinvent-yourself guide. http://www.
barnesandnoble.com/w/reinventing-you-dorie-clark/1112492019?e
an=9781422144138

Karen Kang, *Branding Pays: The Five-Step System to Reinvent Your
Personal Brand,* offers advice about how to improve your personal
brand. http://www.amazon.com/BrandingPays-Five-Step-System-

Reinvent-Personal/dp/0988437503/ref=sr_1_2?s=books&ie=UTF8&
qid=1369572637&sr=1-2&keywords=personal+branding

Websites

http://www.mlive.com/jobs/index.ssf/2010/11/survey_concludes_
that_personal_branding.html

http://www.stevepavlina.com/blog/2008/02/personal-branding/

http://www.quintcareers.com/branding_self-marketing.html

Personal Appearance

Books

Tim Gunn and Kate Moloney, *Tim Gunn: A Guide to Quality, Taste
and Style (Tim Gunn's Guide to Style),* provides useful, entertaining
suggestions about how to find your personal style. http://books.
google.com/books/about/Tim_Gunn.html?id=AmbGvh9q_6YC

Websites

http://www.exforsys.com/career-center/job-search-tips/your-
personal-appearance-can-help-you-land-a-job.html

http://youlookfab.com/2010/04/29/what-to-wear-to-a-job-interview/

http://jobs.aol.com/articles/2011/09/08/what-to-wear-and-not-to-
wear-to-an-interview-infographic/

http://www.quintcareers.com/dressing_at_the_interview.html

http://jobsearch.about.com/od/interviewsnetworking/a/
dressforsuccess.htm

http://jobsearch.about.com/od/interviewattire/a/interviewdress.htm

http://career-advice.monster.com/job-interview/Interview-Appearance/What-to-Wear-for-Job-Interviews/article.aspx

http://angelaharris.hubpages.com/hub/Best-Colors-to-Wear-to-an-Interview

http://jobsearch.about.com/od/interviewattire/a/interviewnot.htm

Mastering the Social Graces

Books

John Bridges, *How to Be a Gentleman,* is a guide to common sense and courtesy. http://johnbridges.com/; http://www.barnesandnoble.com/w/how-to-be-a-gentleman-john-bridges/1110787258?e an=9781401604738

John Bridges and Bryan Curtis, *As a Gentleman Would Say,* offers suggestions for what to say and what not to say in social situations. http://www.amazon.com/Gentleman-Would-Say-Responses-Situations/dp/1558538461

Peggy Post, Anna Post, Lizzie Post, and Daniel Post Senning, *Emily Post's Etiquette, 18th ed.,* is a social-behavior guide for people of all ages who want to comport themselves appropriately in the workplace and in their personal lives. http://www.amazon.com/Emily-Posts-Etiquette-18-ebook/dp/B00512MB3Q

Peggy Post and Peter Post, *Emily Post's The Etiquette Advantage in Business: Personal Skills for Professional Success, Second Edition,* addresses business etiquette topics. http://www.amazon.com/gp/product/0060760028?ie=UTF8&tag=emilypostcom-20&linkCode=as2&camp=1789&creative=9325&creativeASIN=0060760028

Sheryl Shade, *As a Lady Would Say,* offers suggestions about how a lady should respond to specific situations and what she should never say. http://www.barnesandnoble.com/w/as-a-lady-would-say-sheryl-shade/1115205349?ean=9781401604578

Candace Simpson-Giles, *How to Be a Lady,* is a guide to common sense and courtesy. http://www.amazon.com/How-Be-Lady-Contemporary-Courtesy/dp/161375082X

Websites

http://friendship.about.com/od/Friendship_Definitions/g/Social-Grace.htm

http://www.ehow.com/info_8148857_importance-manners-politeness-workplace.html

http://etiquette.about.com/

http://living.msn.com/life-inspired/miss-manners-advice/

http://email.about.com/od/emailnetiquette/tp/core_netiquette.htm

Networking

http://www.forbes.com/sites/susanadams/2011/06/07/networking-is-still-the-best-way-to-find-a-job-survey-says/

http://blogs.hbr.org/cs/2013/02/younger_workers_need_a_career_narrative.html

http://career-advice.monster.com/job-search/professional-networking/jobs.aspx

http://www.enetsc.com/JobSearchTips14.htm

http://jobsearch.about.com/cs/networking/a/networking.htm

http://jobsearch.about.com/od/networking/a/networkingtips.htm

http://www.quintcareers.com/tips/career_networking_tips.html

http://www.helpguide.org/life/job_networking_how_to_find_job.htm

http://money.usnews.com/money/blogs/outside-voices-careers/2011/10/18/6-networking-tips-for-your-job-search

http://www.rileyguide.com/network.html

http://www.cvtips.com/career_advice_forum/blog.php?featured=503&do=list&page=3

http://gethiredfast.com/2012/06/how-to-find-a-job-tell-people-youre-looking/

Social Media/Networking

http://blogs.findlaw.com/official_findlaw_blog/2013/06/tips-for-managing-your-career-on-social-media.html; http://company.findlaw.com/press-center/2013/tips-for-managing-your-career-on-social-media.html; http://www.fox54.com/story/22398844/tips-for-managing-your-career-on-social-media

http://www.cvtips.com/career_advice_forum/entries/501-Conducting-a-Job-Search-With-New-Technology-The-Benefits-of-Social-Media

http://finance.yahoo.com/news/pf_article_109267.html

http://jobsearch.about.com/od/networking/a/socialmedia.htm

http://www.bankrate.com/finance/personal-finance/5-networking-strategies-to-a-new-job-1.aspx

Telephone Interviews

http://www.ehow.com/way_5374212_telephone-interview-tips.html

http://www.quintcareers.com/phone_interviewing-dos-donts.html

http://career-advice.monster.com/job-interview/interview-preparation/mastering-the-phone-interview/article.aspx

http://jobsearch.about.com/cs/interviews/a/phoneinterview.htm

http://video.about.com/jobsearch/Phone-Interview-Tips.htm

Interviewing

http://jobsearch.about.com/od/interviewquestionsanswers/a/interviewquest.htm

http://jobsearch.about.com/od/interviews/tp/jobinterviewtips.htm

http://www.inc.com/jeff-haden/3-interview-questions-that-reveal-everything.html?nav=featured

http://jobs.aol.com/articles/2013/04/17/interview-mistakes-tips/

http://www.stumbleupon.com/su/9dL3v0/jobmob.co.il/blog/sample-job-interview-questions/

http://www.quintcareers.com/learn_about_company.html

http://career-advice.monster.com/job-interview/careers.aspx

http://jobsearch.about.com/cs/interviews/a/aceinterview.htm

http://www.careercc.com/interv3.shtml

http://www.theladders.com/career-advice/interviewing

http://humanresources.about.com/od/interviewing/Interviewing_Tips_and_Interviewing_Techniques.htm

http://www.glassdoor.com/blog/12-ways-blow-job-interview/

http://www.quintcareers.com/acing_behavioral_interview.html

http://www.quintcareers.com/behavioral_interviewing.html

http://www.quintcareers.com/job_interview_follow-up.html

http://www.quintcareers.com/interviewing_articles.html

http://www.cvtips.com/career_advice_forum/entries/487-Five-tips-for-acing-an-interview

http://www.fins.com/Finance/Articles/SB129416698193872447/Top-Ten-Ways-to-Blow-a-Job-Interview

http://finance.yahoo.com/news/10-surefire-ways-blow-job-080105408.html

Cover Letters

http://jobsearch.about.com/od/coverletters/Cover_Letters.htm

http://jobsearch.about.com/od/coverlettersamples/a/coverlettsample.htm

http://www.cover-letters.com/Cover-Letters/About-Cover-Letters/How-To-Write-A-Great-Letter.aspx

http://www.theladders.com/career-advice/showcase-your-personal-brand-in-cover-letter

http://www.nothingbutcoverletters.com/professional-cover-letter-sample.html

http://career-advice.monster.com/résumés-cover-letters/careers.aspx

Résumés

Book

Ellen Gordon Reeves, *Can I Wear My Nose Ring to the Interview? The Crash Course—Finding, Landing and Keeping Your First Job,* is written by a résumé expert and covers, among other things, the do's and don'ts of résumé writing and cover letters. http://www.amazon.com/Can-Wear-Nose-Ring-Interview/dp/0761141456 http://www.amazon.com/Can-Wear-Nose-Ring-Interview/dp/0761141456

Websites

http://www.careercc.com/resumpr.shtml

http://jobsearch.about.com/od/résumés/a/résumégap.htm

http://jobsearch.about.com/od/résumés/u/résumésandletters.htm

http://jobsearch.about.com/od/samplerésumés/a/samplerésumé2.htm

http://www.cvtips.com/career_advice_forum/entries/499-5-Tips-for-Building-a-Résumé

http://jobsearch.about.com/od/résumés/Résumés.htm

http://career-advice.monster.com/résumés-cover-letters/careers.aspx

http://www.cvtips.com/career_advice_forum/entries/407-Put-Volunteer-Work-on-Your-Résumé

http://www.cvtips.com/career_advice_forum/entries/386-3-Résumé-No-No-s

http://jobsearch.about.com/od/résumés/u/résumésandletters.htm#s1

http://jobsearch.about.com/od/résumés/u/résumésandletters.htm#s3

Thank-You Letters

http://blogs.hbr.org/cs/2013/02/how_to_give_a_meaningful_thank.
html

http://career-advice.monster.com/job-interview/following-up/
sample-interview-thank-you-letter/article.aspx

http://jobsearchtech.about.com/od/résumésandletters/tp/Interview_
Thank_Yous.htm

http://jobsearch.about.com/od/résumés/u/résumésandletters.htm#s8

http://www.career.vt.edu/Interviewing/AfterThanksFollowUp.html

Job Offers

Book

Mika Brzezinski, *Knowing Your Value: Women, Money and Getting
What You're Worth,* looks at how women achieve recognition and
compensation parity through the author's personal experience and
interviews with prominent women. http://www.barnesandnoble.
com/w/knowing-your-value-mika-brzezinski/1100227602?e
an=9781602861602

Websites

http://careerplanning.about.com/cs/joboffers/a/evaluate_offer.htm

http://www.ehow.com/negotiating-a-job-offer/

http://www.washingtonpost.com/wp-dyn/content/
discussion/2008/11/06/DI2008110601372.html

http://www.life123.com/career-money/career-development/
negotiating-salary/negotiating-salary-2.shtml

http://www.careerbliss.com/advice/5-tips-for-negotiating-
compensation/

http://www.careerbuilder.com/Article/CB-1333-Interview-Tips-Five-
Ways-to-Negotiate-a-Better-Job-Offer-Despite-the-Economy/

http://money.usnews.com/money/blogs/outside-voices-
careers/2012/04/04/7-tried-and-true-steps-for-negotiating-a-job-
offer

http://jobsearch.about.com/od/salaryinformation/tp/salary-
negotiation-strategies.htm

http://www.rileyguide.com/offers.html

http://jobsearch.about.com/b/2013/05/12/how-to-negotiate-a-job-
offer.htm

http://www.quintcareers.com/salary_negotiation.html

Career Planning and Advice

Websites

http://www.businessweek.com/articles/2013-04-23/the-new-rules-
for-the-modern-workplace

http://www.ehow.com/how_8516434_make-career-happen.html

http://medixstaffingsolutions.blogspot.com/2011/12/how-to-break-
up-with-your-job-properly.html

http://www.life123.com/career-money/career-development/
negotiating-salary/negotiating-salary-2.shtml

http://money.usnews.com/money/blogs/outside-voices-careers/2011/05/10/16-signs-its-time-to-quit-your-job

http://gethiredfast.com/2012/06/how-to-find-a-job-when-you-already-have-one/

http://jobsearch.about.com/od/joblistings/tp/jobbanks.htm

http://www.careerpath.com/resources/

Promotions

http://www.cvtips.com/career_advice_forum/entries/473-What-Does-it-Take-to-Get-Promoted

http://jobsearch.about.com/od/jobpromotions/a/how-to-get-a-promotion.htm

http://www.career-success-for-newbies.com/how-to-get-promoted.html

http://www.lifeaftercollege.org/blog/2010/04/29/promotions/

http://www.huffingtonpost.com/learnvest/how-to-get-promoted_b_1682977.html?view=print&comm_ref=false

http://suite101.com/article/how-to-get-a-promotion-a27942

http://www.quintcareers.com/getting_promoted_strategies.html

http://www.cbsnews.com/8301-505125_162-57261230/career-advice-how-to-get-promoted/

Managing Workplace Issues

http://management.fortune.cnn.com/2013/04/23/bullying-cruelty-work-office/

http://www.howtohaveabullyfreeworkplace.com

http://www.washingtonpost.com/blogs/on-leadership/
wp/2013/05/20/why-bullies-succeed-at-work-2/

http://www.fastcompany.com/3006749/how-bounce-back-stronger-
after-you-blow-it-work

http://www.marketwatch.com/story/is-your-company-watching-
your-weight-2013-02-25

http://www.cbsnews.com/8301-505125_162-57571587/does-
telecommuting-hurt-your-career/

http://www.usatoday.com/story/money/columnist/
bruzzese/2013/03/10/on-the-job-email-clarity/1972443/

http://money.usnews.com/money/blogs/outside-voices-
careers/2013/02/19/how-to-get-on-your-bosss-good-side-without-
brown-nosing

http://money.usnews.com/money/blogs/outside-voices-
careers/2013/02/14/your-job-sucks-here-are-10-reasons-to-love-it-
anyway

http://money.usnews.com/money/blogs/outside-voices-
careers/2013/02/14/these-5-workplace-habits-are-making-you-look-
amateur

http://jobs.aol.com/articles/2013/02/20/appearance-
discrimination/?a_dgi=aolshare_twitter

http://money.usnews.com/money/blogs/outside-voices-
careers/2013/02/21/how-to-get-along-with-a-dreadful-boss

http://www.careerbliss.com/advice/4-ways-for-young-professionals-
to-maintain-motivation/

http://www.cvtips.com/career_advice_forum/entries/420-Cliques-in-the-Workplace

http://www.careerbliss.com/advice/4-tips-for-millennials-to-work-well-with-boomers/

Employee Benefits

http://www.ehow.com/info_8100708_employee-assistance.html

http://www.netplaces.com/money-for-20s-30s/show-me-the-money-work-and-career/employee-ownership-plans.htm;

http://stocks.about.com/od/investingtechniques/a/emplstoc102004.htm

http://employeeissues.com/i_employee_benefits.htm

http://humanresources.about.com/od/glossaryt/g/tuition.htm

Persons with Disabilities

Book

Daniel J. Ryan, *Job Search Handbook for People with Disabilities,* is a career planning and job search guide for people with disabilities. http://www.amazon.com/Job-Search-Handbook-People-Disabilities/dp/1563709899

Websites

http://blog.nwjobs.com/careercenterblog/2011/03/interviewing-tips-for-people-w.html

http://www.provenrésumés.com/disable.html

http://jobsearch.about.com/b/2011/02/14/job-searching-tips-for-people-with-disabilities.htm

http://www.quintcareers.com/disabled_career_resources.html

http://www.rileyguide.com/abled.html

http://career-advice.monster.com/résumés-cover-letters/careers.aspx

http://abilityrésumé.com/

http://career-advice.monster.com/job-search/getting-started/5-tips-for-jobhunting-with-a-disability-hot-jobs/article.aspx

http://work.chron.com/job-interview-tips-people-disabilities-6998.html

http://www.learningrx.com/quotes-from-famous-people-with-learning-disabilities-faq.htm

http://www.disabled-world.com/artman/publish/article_0060.shtml

http://yeswecanbahamas.webs.com/quotesbypersonswithdisabilities.htm

Veterans

http://www.rileyguide.com/vets.html

http://jobs.aol.com/articles/2011/01/18/cover-letters-for-career-changers/

http://www.jobsinmanhattan.com/articles/title/Best-Practices-in-Résumé-Writing-For-Veterans/3678/424

www.veteranemployment.com

http://www.militaryhire.com/loginvalidate.servlet

http://www.hireveterans.com/

http://www.inc.com/randy-stover/why-i-only-hire-veterans.html

http://www.hireheroesusa.org/hire-a-veteran/why-hire-a-veteran/

http://www.veteranstoday.com/2010/01/25/10-top-reasons-to-hire-veterans/

http://jobsearch.about.com/od/veterans/a/veteran-job-search.htm

Federal Labor and Employment Law Topics and Employment-Related Legal Issues

The laws cited here are not an exhaustive list of all federal laws impacting employees and employers. This is only a list of some of those laws.

Current Laws

Federal Labor–Management Legislative Framework

National Labor Relations Act (NLRA)—The federal law that established the National Labor Relations Board (NLRB) and limits the means by which employers may react to workers in the private sector who organize labor unions, engage in collective bargaining, and take part in strikes and other forms of concerted activity in support of their demands. The NLRA does not cover those workers who are subject to the **Railway Labor Act**; agricultural employees; domestic employees; supervisors; federal, state, or local government workers; independent contractors; and some close relatives of individual employers.

Taft-Hartley Act—This legislation amended the NLRA and established control of labor disputes on a new basis by enlarging the NLRB and providing that the union or the employer must, before terminating a collective bargaining agreement, serve notice on the other party and on a government mediation service. The government was empowered to obtain an eighty-day injunction against any strike that it deemed a peril to national health or safety. **Landrum–Griffin Act**

(also known by its official name, the Labor Management Reporting and Disclosure Act) is legislation that was passed in 1959 to deal with the relationship between unions and their members. This legislation established a bill of rights for union members and requires that unions follow democratic procedures. https://www.nlrb.gov/national-labor-relations-act

Civil Rights Act of 1964 (Title VII)—Prohibits discrimination (including harassment and retaliation) because of race, color, sex, religion, and national origin. http://www.dol.gov/dol/topic/discrimination/ethnicdisc.htm

Pregnancy Discrimination Act of 1964 (PDA)—Prohibits discrimination based on pregnancy when it comes to any aspect of employment, including hiring, firing, pay, job assignments, promotions, layoff, training, fringe benefits, such as leave and health insurance, and any other term or condition of employment. http://www.eeoc.gov/laws/types/pregnancy.cfm

Age Discrimination in Employment Act (ADEA)—Prohibits discrimination against individuals age 40 and over; **Older Workers Benefits Protection Act (OWBPA)**—In 1990, Congress passed this act that amended the ADEA to safeguard older workers' employee benefits from age discrimination. http://www.dol.gov/dol/topic/discrimination/agedisc.htm#lawregs; http://www.eeoc.gov/facts/age.html

Americans with Disabilities Act of 1990 and the Rehabilitation Act of 1973—Both statutes prohibit discrimination against individuals with physical or mental disabilities. http://www.dol.gov/dol/topic/discrimination/disabilitydisc.htm

Americans with Disabilities Act Amendments Act (ADAAA)—Expanded the definition of a disability to make it easier to prove that someone is disabled; added new "major life activities," including eating, sleeping, bending, reading, concentrating, thinking, communicating and major bodily functions. http://www.eeoc.gov/laws/statutes/adaaa_info.cfm

Equal Pay Act (EPA)—Prohibits gender-based discrimination in compensation for equal work. The **Lilly Ledbetter Fair Pay Act of 2009** allows pay discrimination claims to be filed within 180 or 300 days (depending on the filing jurisdiction) of the issuance of the discriminatory paycheck. http://www.eeoc.gov/laws/statutes/epa.cfm

Fair Labor Standards Act (FLSA)—Federal law that governs wage and hour issues. http://www.dol.gov/whd/flsa/

Family and Medical Leave Act (FMLA)—Requires covered employers to provide twelve weeks of job-protected, unpaid leave to eligible employees for qualifying events. http://www.dol.gov/whd/fmla/

Immigration Reform and Control Act (IRCA)—Designed to help control illegal immigration to the United States; requires employers to assure that employees hired are legally authorized to work in the United States. Under IRCA, it is illegal to hire or recruit illegal immigrants knowingly (i.e., immigrants who do not possess lawful work authorization). It also requires employers to attest to their employees' immigration status and grants amnesty to certain illegal immigrants who entered the United States before January 1, 1982, and have resided there continuously; see also http://www.dol.gov/dol/topic/discrimination/immdisc.htm.

Employee Retirement Income Security Act (ERISA)—Federal law that sets minimum standards for most voluntarily established pension and health plans in private industry to provide protection for individuals in these plans. http://www.dol.gov/compliance/laws/comp-erisa.htm

Uniformed Services Employment and Reemployment Rights Act (USERRA)—Guarantees re-employment rights to eligible employees who leave their jobs to enter military service. http://www.dol.gov/compliance/laws/comp-userra.htm

Occupational Safety and Health Administration (OSHA)—OSHA's role is to assure safe and healthy working conditions for workers by authorizing enforcement of the standards developed under the Occupational Safety and Health Act. https://www.osha.gov/

Worker Adjustment and Retraining Notification Act (WARN)—Requires covered employers to provide advance notice to employees of closings and layoffs. http://www.dol.gov/compliance/laws/comp-warn-regs.htm

Fair Credit Reporting Act (FCRA)—Designed to promote accuracy and insure the privacy of the information used in consumer credit reports, including background checks. http://www.ftc.gov/os/statutes/031224fcra.pdf

Executive Order 11246—Prohibits federal contractors and subcontractors and federally assisted construction contractors and subcontractors that generally have contracts that exceed $10,000 from discriminating in employment decisions on the basis of race, color, religion, sex, or national origin. It also requires that covered contractors take affirmative action to insure that equal opportunity is provided in all aspects of their employment. http://www.dol.gov/compliance/laws/comp-eeo.htm

Vietnam Era Veterans' Readjustment Assistance Act (VEVRAA)—Requires that covered federal government contractors and subcontractors take affirmative action to employ and advance in employment specified categories of veterans protected by the act, and prohibits discrimination against such veterans. In addition, VEVRAA requires contractors and subcontractors to list their employment openings with the appropriate employment service delivery system, and that covered veterans receive priority in referral to such openings. http://www.dol.gov/compliance/laws/comp-vevraa.htm

Consolidated Omnibus Budget Reconciliation Act (COBRA)—Gives workers and their families, who lose their health benefits, the right to choose to continue group health benefits provided by their group health plan for limited periods of time under certain circumstances, such as voluntary or involuntary job loss; reduction in the hours worked; transition between jobs, death, or divorce; and other life events. Qualified individuals may be required to pay the entire premium for coverage up to 102 percent of the cost of the plan. http://www.dol.gov/dol/topic/health-plans/cobra.htm

Health Insurance Portability and Accountability Act of 1996 (HIPAA)—Privacy and Security Rules provide federal protections for personal health information held by covered entities, and gives patients an array of rights with respect to that information. At the same time, the Privacy Rule is balanced, so that it permits the disclosure of personal health information needed for patient care and other important purposes. The Security Rule specifies a series of administrative, physical, and technical safeguards for covered entities to use to assure the confidentiality, integrity, and availability of protected electronic health information. http://www.hhs.gov/ocr/privacy/hipaa/understanding/index.html

Privacy Act—Protects records that can be retrieved by personal identifiers, such as a name, Social Security number, or other identifying number or symbol. http://www.ssa.gov/privacyact.htm

Endnotes

1.   Additional links to third-party websites were added in May and August 2013, and were accessible as of the date of the material.

2.   The selected quotations are included because of their message. Where a specific gender is referenced, please substitute the pronoun considered appropriate.

3.   President Barack Obama's State of the Union Address, Jan. 25, 2011.

4.   "The Disposable Worker" by Michelle Conlin, Moira Herbst, and Peter Coy on Jan. 7, 2010. http://www.businessweek.com/magazine/content/10_03/b4163032935448.htm

5.   "How recession changed job market," quoting Roy Cohen, career coach and author of *The Wall Street Professional's Survival Guide*, by Debra Auerbach, Jan. 30, 2012. http://articles.chicagotribune.com/2012-01-30/classified/chi-how-recession-changed-job-market-20120130_1_job-seekers-job-fairs-job-market

6.   http://www.whatissocialnetworking.com/

7.   "Tell-All Generation Learns to Keep Things Offline" by Laura M. Holson, *The New York Times*, May 8, 2010, including a quote by Mary Madden, a senior research specialist for the Pew Internet Project. http://www.pewinternet.org/Media-Mentions/2010/Tell-All-Generation-Learns-to-Keep-Things-Offline.aspx; http://www.nytimes.com/2010/05/09/fashion/09privacy.html

8.   Ibid.

9. "6 Career-Killing Facebook Mistakes" by Erin Joyce, Managing Editor, *Yahoo Finance News*, Apr. 7, 2010. http://finance.yahoo.com/news/pf_article_109267.html

10. http://www.emilypost.com/etiquette-18th-edition

11. John Bridges, *How to Be a Gentleman Revised & Updated: A Contemporary Guide to Common Courtesy (GentleManners)*, Nashville, TN: Rutledge Hill Press (2012)

12. Candace Simpson-Giles, *How to Be a Lady Revised & Updated: A Contemporary Guide to Common Courtesy (GentleManners)*, Nashville, TN: Thomas Nelson (2012)

13. John Bridges and Bryan Curtis, *As a Gentleman Would Say: Responses to Life's Important (and Sometimes Awkward) Situations (GentleManners)*, Nashville, TN: Rutledge Hill Press (2012)

14. Sheryl Shade, *As a Lady Would Say Revised & Updated: Responses to Life's Important (and Sometimes Awkward) Situations (GentleManners)*, Nashville, TN: Thomas Nelson (2012)

15. "Survey Concludes that Personal Branding is the Key to Job Opportunities" by Jackie Headapohl. http://www.mlive.com/jobs/index.ssf/2010/11/survey_concludes_that_personal_branding.html

16. "Personal Branding" by Steve Pavlina. http://www.stevepavlina.com/blog/2008/02/personal-branding/

17. http://www.buzzle.com/articles/personality-traits-list.html

18. http://careerplanning.about.com/cs/aboutassessment/a/assess_overview.htm

19. http://www.onetonline.org/

20. "The Less You Associate with Some People the More Your Life Will Improve" by Colin Powell. http://www.goodreads.com/

quotes/310930-the-less-you-associate-with-some-people-the-more-your

21. Given the competition for jobs, some elementary, middle, and high schools may favor candidates who have a graduate degree.

22. Thanks to Martha Sloane, Principal, MARTHA SLOANE CONSULTANTS, LTD, A Recruiting Firm, Falls Village, CT, for her contribution to this section.

23. http://www.ada.gov/employmt.htm. An excerpt from "ADA Questions and Answers." http://www.ada.gov/qandaeng.htm by the U.S. Equal Employment Opportunity Commission and the U.S. Department of Justice.

24. http://www.disabled-world.com/artman/publish/article_0060.shtml

25. "The Disposable Worker" by Michelle Conlin, Moira Herbst, and Peter Coy on Jan. 07, 2010. http://www.businessweek.com/magazine/content/10_03/b4163032935448.htm

26. Ibid.

27. The three methods are: 1) Exclusion under federal law; 2) Validation under the Uniform Guide on Employee Selection Procedures; or 3) Targeted Screens and Individualized Assessments.

28. EEOC Enforcement Guidance dated April 25, 2012, Section V, subsection B-2. http://www.eeoc.gov/laws/guidance/arrest_conviction.cfm

29. Carter G. Woodson, *The Mis-Education of the Negro* [January 2005], first published by The Associated Publishers in 1933. http://www.goodreads.com/work/quotes/235359-the-mis-education-of-the-negro; http://www.amazon.com/Miseducation-Negro-Carter-Godwin-Woodson/dp/1564110419#reader_1564110419

30. Leslie A. Geddes, ME, PhD, FACC, FRSM, Showalter Distinguished Professor Emeritus of Biomedical Engineering, Purdue University.

31. http://www.howtohaveabullyfreeworkplace.com

32. Adapted from Laura Deaton, cofounder of ThirdSectorConnector. org. Reprinted with permission from Third Sector Connector, © 2010. Reprinted with permission from Ms. Deaton.

33. CBS-TV, *60 Minutes*, May 25, 2007, "The 'Millennials' Are Coming, Morley Safer on The New Generation Of American Workers." www. cbsnews.com/stories/2007/11/08/60minutes/main3475200.shtml.

34. Helicopter parents are so named because they hover over their children.

35. Thanks to Adrienne Colotti for her substantial contribution to this section.

36. http://www.relationship-affairs.com/Employer-Employee-Relationships.html

37. "Tuition Assistance" by Susan M. Heathfield, About.com Guide. http://humanresources.about.com/od/glossaryt/g/tuition.htm

38. http://www.ehow.com/info_8100708_employee-assistance.html

39. http://www.netplaces.com/money-for-20s-30s/show-me-the-money-work-and-career/employee-ownership-plans.htm; http://stocks.about. com/od/investingtechniques/a/emplstoc102004.htm

40. http://stocks.about.com/od/investingtechniques/a/emplstoc102004. htm

41. http://www.investorwords.com/11/401k_plan.html

42. The laws cited in this chapter are not an exhaustive list of all federal laws impacting employees and employers. This is only a list of some of those laws, and is provided for informational purposes only.

43. ReconsiDer is a New York not-for-profit organization, which provides a forum for discussing the war on drugs.

44. "What Enron, WorldCom, Tyco Fiascos Can Teach Us" by John Dorfman on Mar. 2, 2004. http://www.bloomberg.com/apps/news?pid =newsarchive&sid=aqrJ2Fj0XJj0

45. "Amazon, Big Six Sued by Independent Bookstores Over DRM" by Mercy Pilkington. http://goodereader.com/blog/electronic-readers/ amazon-big-six-sued-by-independent-bookstores-over-drm/

46. http://www.justice.gov/criminal/fraud/fcpa/guidance/ and a December 2011 client presentation by Lowenstein Sandler, P.C., Roseland, New Jersey

47. http://www.justice.gov/atr/about/antitrust-laws.html

48. Leslie A. Geddes, ME, PhD, FACC, FRSM, Showalter Distinguished Professor Emeritus of Biomedical Engineering, Purdue University

49. Dr. Margaret C. Harrell and Nancy Berglass

50. Lady Gaga on "Mastering the Art of Fame," 60 Minutes, February 13, 2011.

51. "Oprah Presents Master Class with Jay-Z," Jan. 9, 2011.

52. The third-party websites are identified for your convenience, and are not maintained by Parthenon Enterprises, Inc. Accordingly, access to these websites is subject to the third parties' discretion and their decision to make the material available.

Index

C

Y

About the Author

Photo by www.dwightcarter.com

BEVERLY A. WILLIAMS is an attorney, legal consultant, and lecturer, who specializes in employment and labor law issues. She teaches seminars in Rutgers University's School of Management and Labor Relations, and Center for Management Development, and conducts employment-skills workshops for people of all ages.

Beverly served as Vice President of Automatic Data Processing, Inc.'s Corporate Employment Law Services Department, which provided advice and counsel about employment law and labor matters to the company's C-Suite executives, HR professionals, and sales and service management.

Prior to joining the corporate world, Beverly was associated with Epstein Becker Green, P.C., in the firm's New York City and Newark, New Jersey, offices. During this time, she served as a regular employment law guest anchor on Tru TV, formerly known as Court TV.

Beverly had the privilege of serving as Law Secretary to the Honorable Robert N. Wilentz, Chief Justice, Supreme Court of New Jersey, during the term in which the Baby M case was decided. Prior to being admitted to the bar, Beverly held various HR positions, including Executive Director of Labor Relations for the Newark, New Jersey, School District.

She received her juris doctorate from Rutgers School of Law, Newark, New Jersey, where she was an editor of the *Rutgers Law Review*. Beverly received a Master of Public Administration from the University of North Carolina at Chapel Hill as a Ford Foundation Fellowship recipient, and attended Douglass College, Rutgers University, where she received a B.A. in Political Science.

She is admitted to the bars of the State of New Jersey, the District of Columbia Court of Appeals, and several Federal District Court Bars. She is a member of the American Bar Association (Labor & Employment and Litigation Sections), the New Jersey State Bar Association, and the District of Columbia Bar Association.

More of What People Are Saying about *Get the Job · Done* ✓

Get the Job • Done ✓ *is a much-needed resource that provides an advantage for inexperienced job seekers, including returning veterans, people with disabilities, and anyone interested in enhancing their employment experience. Whether you are entering the job market for the first time or returning after some time off, there is something here for you, including practical tips and resources on how to interview, how to dress, and how to write a cover letter that distinguishes you from the competition. This book can show you how to become the person that prospective employers want to hire or promote.*

—Wade Henderson, President and CEO, The Leadership Conference on Civil and Human Rights and The Leadership Conference Education Fund

The material in this book offered me employment advice as do's and don'ts, tips, stories, and cautionary tales, and saved me time by also identifying numerous Internet resources that proved helpful in my job search. Following certain tips made all the difference to my approach to interviews and a successful placement. Get the Job • Done ✓ *is a guide and resource that empowers job seekers.*

—Kavita Aggarwal, accountant

Beverly Williams's book is a practical, straightforward roadmap to finding your next job. The reader will have the advantage of her years of Human Resources expertise and employer insight. How to wow at interviews, proper dress etiquette, and the do's and don'ts of on-the-job relationships are just a few of the topics covered here. Get the Job • Done ✓ *will arm you with all the information and confidence you'll need to go out and get the career you've always wanted.*

—Maria Tabone, holistic health educator and author, *The Holistic Root to Managing Anxiety*

Made in the USA
Charleston, SC
15 January 2015